Sports Law in Hong Kong

Sports Law in Hong Kong

Nick Chan Hiu-Fung
Hin Han Shum
Sylvia Tsang

This book was originally published as a monograph in the International Encyclopaedia of Laws/Sports Law.

Founding Editor: Roger Blanpain
General Editor: Frank Hendrickx
Volume Editor: Michele Colucci

Wolters Kluwer

Published by:
Kluwer Law International B.V.
PO Box 316
2400 AH Alphen aan den Rijn
The Netherlands
E-mail: lrs-sales@wolterskluwer.com
Website: www.wolterskluwer.com/en/solutions/kluwerlawinternational

Sold and distributed by:
Wolters Kluwer Legal & Regulatory U.S.
920 Links Avenue
Landisville, PA 17538
United States of America
E-mail: customer.service@wolterskluwer.com

ISBN 978-94-035-3089-5

e-Book: ISBN 978-94-035-3099-4
web-PDF: ISBN 978-94-035-3109-0

The Author

Nick Chan Hiu-Fung, BBS, MH, JP, Hon Fellow (HKUST), HKIArb (Fellow), an interdisciplinary lawyer and lawmaker with a computer science background, is a Partner at international law firm Squire Patton Boggs. He holds a Bachelor of Laws and Bachelor of Science (Computer Science) from The University of Melbourne.

Mr. Chan is the Director leading the operations of AALCO Hong Kong Regional Arbitration Centre which is established by international law and has the support of forty-nine member countries. The Centre leads in sports dispute resolution services and training in the region. The Hong Kong SAR Government recognized Mr. Chan's public and community services with a Bronze Bauhinia Star, Medal of Honor and appointed him as a Justice of the Peace. The Hong Kong University of Science and Technology has awarded Mr. Chan with an Honorary Fellowship in 2023. Mr. Chan is an elected and serving Hong Kong Deputy to the National People's Congress.

Mr. Chan teaches law at the City University of Hong Kong. He gives guest lectures at Peking University, Tsing Hua University, and The University of Hong Kong. He serves on the law school boards for The University of Hong Kong, the Chinese University of Hong Kong, and the City University of Hong Kong. He chaired the Sports and Recreation Committee of The Law Society of Hong Kong and served as a board member of The Recreation and Sports Club for Hong Kong Professional Bodies.

Mr. Chan is deeply passionate about sport and actively participates in various sporting events and initiatives. He serves as the Honorary Legal Advisor and Chairperson of the Election Committee for the Sports Federation & Olympic Committee of Hong Kong, China, as Board Member of the Sports Association for Older Adults in Hong Kong, China Limited, as Board Member and Chairman of the Legal Committee for The Football Association of Hong Kong, China Limited (HKFA), as Board Member for the Squash Association of Hong Kong, China, and as Observer on the Board for the Karatedo Federation of Hong Kong, China Limited. Mr. Chan also serves as the Honorary Legal Advisor for the Hong Kong Chess Federation Limited and the Hong Kong Darts Federation.

The Author

Co-Authors

Hin Han Shum is a solicitor advocate, prosecutor on fiat, and accredited general mediator. She is also empaneled as an arbitrator of the Asian-African Legal Consultative Organization (AALCO). She formerly sat on the Steering Committee on Mediation under the Department of Justice and is admitted as an associate member of the Hong Kong Institute of Arbitrators.

She serves in the Telecommunications, Media and Technology, Litigation, and Sports and Entertainment law practice groups of Squire Patton Boggs. She has been seconded to international companies to assist their in-house legal teams with day-to-day operations and major legal transactions, where she has enhanced her ability to develop pragmatic approaches to solve business operation issues. She utilizes knowledge gained from her litigation practice to mitigate dispute risks at the contract drafting stage for commercial transactions.

Ms. Shum currently sits on the Council of the Law Society of Hong Kong (the regulatory body of all Hong Kong solicitors) and serves as a member of various committees, including the Standing Committee on Compliance and External Affairs, Sports Law Committee, Anti-Money Laundering Committee, Innotech Committee, Arbitration Committee and Mediation Committee. She is currently an officer of the International Bar Association (IBA) Young Lawyers Committee and Anti-Corruption Committee.

She has guest lectured at Peking University, Beijing Jiaotong University, Paris 1 Panthéon-Sorbonne University, and the University of Hong Kong. She is often invited to speak at international conferences and organizations on topics including mergers and acquisitions, artificial intelligence in businesses, blockchain, data privacy, international commercial arbitration, and art law, and has contributed to the "Annotated Ordinances of Hong Kong: Business Registration Ordinance" (Cap. 310) (3rd edition, published by LexisNexis), the Partnership Law Handbook (3rd edition, published by LexisNexis) and other research projects conducted by the World Bank.

She is a Chairperson of the Appeal Tribunal Panel (Buildings) and sits on Criminal and Law Enforcement Injuries Compensation Boards.

Co-Authors

Sylvia Tsang is an associate at Squire Patton Boggs. She received a Bachelor of Journalism from the University of Hong Kong, and a Juris Doctor and Postgraduate Certificate in Laws (PCLL) from the City University of Hong Kong.

She is empaneled as a mediator of the AALCO and has made contributions to the "Annotated Ordinances of Hong Kong: Business Registration Ordinance" (Cap. 310) (3rd edition, published by LexisNexis), the Partnership Law Handbook (3rd edition, also published by LexisNexis), as well as various research projects conducted by the World Bank.

Table of Contents

List of Abbreviations

AALCO	Asian-African Legal Consultative Organization
AALCO-HKRAC	AALCO Hong Kong Regional Arbitration Centre
ADR	Alternative Dispute Resolution
AI	Artificial Intelligence
AIAC	Asian International Arbitration Centre
Atari	Atari Incorporated
BPR	Best Practice Reference for Governance of National Sports Associations—Towards Excellence in Sports Professional Development
Bulletin	Competition Commission Advisory Bulletin
CADA	Chinese Anti-doping Agency
CAS	Court of Arbitration for Sport
CCAS	China Commission of Arbitration for Sport
COVID-19	Coronavirus Disease 2019
CPI(A)	Headline Consumer Price Index (A)
CSTB	Culture, Sports and Tourism Bureau
CULF	Conditions of Use of LCSD Recreation and Sports Facilities
DTA	Comprehensive Double Taxation Agreement
eBRAM	eBRAM International Online Dispute Resolution Centre Limited
EO	Employment Ordinance (Cap. 57)
e-sports	Electronic Sports
EU	European Union
EVSS	Government's Elite Vote Support Scheme
FFAR	Football Agent Regulations
FIFA	Fédération Internationale de Football Association
GDP	Gross Domestic Product
GDPR	General Data Protection Regulation
GEP	General Employment Policy

List of Abbreviations

HK Cable	Hong Kong Cable Television Ltd
HKAAA	Hong Kong, China Association of Athletics Affiliates
HKADC	Hong Kong Anti-doping Committee
HKBA	Badminton Association of Hong Kong, China
HKCFA	Hong Kong Court of Final Appeal
HKFA	The Football Association of Hong Kong, China Limited
HKIAC	Hong Kong International Arbitration Centre
HKIMC	Hong Kong International Mediation Centre
HKJC	Hong Kong Jockey Club
HKRU	Hong Kong China Rugby Union
HKSAR	Hong Kong Special Administrative Region of the People's Republic of China
HKSI	Hong Kong Sports Institute
HKSI CCEC	Hong Kong Sports Institute Coaching Code of Ethical Conduct
HKSI SCEC	Hong Kong Sports Institute Staff Code of Ethical Conduct
HKTA	Hong Kong China Tennis Association
IC	Independent Contractor
ICAC	Independent Commission Against Corruption
IFS	International Sports Federation
Immigration Facilitation Scheme	Immigration Facilitation for Visitors Participating in Short-Term Activities in Designated Sectors
Interim Measures Arrangement	Arrangement Concerning Mutual Assistance in Court-ordered Interim Measures in Aid of Arbitral Proceedings by the Courts of the Mainland and of the Hong Kong
IOC	International Olympic Committee
IRD	Inland Revenue Department
IRO	Inland Revenue Ordinance (Cap. 112)
JCAIAS	Jockey Club Athlete Incentive Awards Scheme
Joint Declaration	Sino-British Joint Declaration on the question of Hong Kong
JSC	Jubilee Sports Centre
LCSD	Leisure and Cultural Services Department
LegCo	Legislative Council
Mediation Convention	United Nations Convention on International Settlement Agreements Resulting From Mediation

New York Convention	United Nations Convention on the Recognition and Enforcement of Foreign Arbitral Awards
NOC	National Olympic Committee(s)
NPC	National People's Congress
NSA	National Sports Association(s)
PCPD	Privacy Commissioner for Personal Data
PDPO	Personal Data (Privacy) Ordinance (Cap. 486)
PGR	Pleasure Grounds Regulation
PIPL	Personal Information Protection Law
POBO	Prevention of Bribery Ordinance (Cap. 201)
PRC/China	People's Republic of China
RAT	Rapid Antigen Test
SC	Sports Commission
SCST	Secretary for Culture, Sports and Tourism
SEP	Sharing Economic Prosperity
SF&OC	Sports Federation & Olympic Committee of Hong Kong, China
TMZ	Trimetazidine
TVB	Television Broadcasts Ltd
UK	United Kingdom
WADA	World Anti-doping Agency
WUMPO	Companies (Winding Up and Miscellaneous Provisions) Ordinance (Cap. 32)

List of Abbreviations

Forewords

I love sports, all kinds of sports. To grow the sports industry, we must improve governance and set fair and common playing fields. It gives me great pleasure and honor to be invited by my dear friend and lead author Nick Chan, who share a common passion to contribute to sports and the sports industry, to write this preface for the Hong Kong chapter of the International Encyclopaedia of Laws: Sports Law, an authoritative guide that provides a great overview of the legal framework and issues pertaining to the sports industry in our beloved city.

Playing sports as a pastime is deeply rooted in the childhood of many people, and it shapes our culture, history, and identity. From winning numerous medals and accolades at the recent 2024 Paris Olympics to staging spectacular mega events such as the Hong Kong Sevens, the Formula E, and the World Championship for Lacrosse U20, our city and residents have demonstrated passion, excellence, diversity and inclusion.

Serving as Hong Kong Deputy to the National People's Congress, Legislative Council lawmaker, and President of the Sports Federation & Olympic Committee of Hong Kong, China, I have witnessed the remarkable evolution of our sports landscape over the years. The Government of the Hong Kong Special Administrative Region, with staunch support from the Central People's Government, has firmly recognized the great importance and potential of sports and invested in people's heath, training, technology, sports facilities and infrastructure. A wide range of fostering policies and initiatives are in place to promote sports participation and development within the community. The Hong Kong Sports Institute (HKSI) has also played a pivotal role in nurturing elite athletes and supporting their pursuit of sporting excellence. Additionally, the private sector, universities and the wider society have contributed significantly to the growth and vibrancy of the sports industry, through sponsorship, partnership, and innovation.

The sports industry also faces challenges and legal issues, particularly relating to intellectual property, liability, and dispute resolution. Addressing these issues requires a sound and robust legal system that balances the interests and rights of different stakeholders, ensures fairness and integrity in sports activities, and provides effective remedies and enforcement mechanisms. The Hong Kong Special Administrative Region enjoys a high degree of autonomy and a very strong rule of law, along with unique advantages under "One Country, Two Systems" to strengthen our leadership as the preeminent international hub for legal services, arbitration and mediation. These factors were greatly strengthened by international developments with the strong vote of confidence and support with the establishment of AALCO

Hong Kong Regional Arbitration Centre by the international inter-government organization Asian-African Legal Consultative Organization (AALCO) with forty-nine countries as Member States, and the establishment of the International Organization for Mediation, for Hong Kong to rise to the next level to offer a conducive and most favorable environment for the development and resolution of sports-related legislation and dispute resolution center for the region, the Global South and beyond.

This publication on Hong Kong's Sports Law serves as a handbook filled with accessible references for anyone interested in the legal aspects of sports in the region. It covers the general background and sources of sports law, the legal framework governing various aspects of sports, such as employment, commerce, tort, and public health and safety, as well as the relationship between natural justice and sports justice. It also examines the current issues and trends affecting the sports industry, including the impact of COVID-19, the rise of electronic sports, and the promotion of equality and inclusion in sports. It draws on the relevant legislation, case law, policies, and practices in Hong Kong, as well as the comparative and international perspectives.

I extend my sincere gratitude and appreciation to the authors of this encyclopedia, for their diligent and professional work in compiling and presenting this valuable resource. I am confident that this book will serve as a useful guide for legal practitioners, academics, students, sports administrators, athletes, and anyone interested in the fascinating and dynamic field of sports law.

Hon Kenneth FOK Kai Kong, JP

I am delighted to know that Hong Kong will have its own Sports Law dedicated encyclopedia and my dear friend and co-director of the Sports Association for Older Adults in Hong Kong, China, is penning this important authoritative go-to guide. I have always been an avid sports fan—athletes exhibit grit, tenacity, determination, skills and stamina to overcome the impossible and break world records and personal best! Sports strengthen and unite us, and are an integral part of societal growth, creating opportunities for cultural exchange, international cooperation, and economic development, while also reflecting the values, history, and identity of a people and a place and the challenges and aspirations we face.

Sports is an integral part of the livelihood in Hong Kong. As one of the world's most international cities in a country with so much history and culture, and with a history of British rule, Hong Kong has a diverse and dynamic sports landscape that combines both Western and Asian elements. From traditional sports to modern e-sports, and from local sports clubs to global mega-events, sports have brought people together from diverse backgrounds. Hong Kong presents a rich array of sports experiences for its residents and visitors.

This book, *The International Encyclopaedia of Laws: Sports Law - Hong Kong*, provides a comprehensive and up-to-date overview of the legal framework and practices of sports in Hong Kong. It covers the sources, institutions, and principles of sports law in Hong Kong, alongside potential opportunities and developments of different types of sports activities and organizations. It also analyzes the current challenges and trends in sports law, as well as the potential opportunities and developments in the future.

As a Legislative Council lawmaker and Vice-chairman of the Hong Kong Sports Institute, I have been actively involved in promoting sports legislation and policy in Hong Kong. I believe that a sound and effective legal system is essential for the sustainable and healthy growth of the sports sector. This, in turn, will allow for the protection and empowerment of the sports community. I have also been advocating for greater support and recognition for our elite athletes, who have brought glory and pride to Hong Kong with their outstanding achievements in international competitions. I have recently proposed several policy recommendations to the government aimed at enhancing Hong Kong's sports governance and support for athletes, such as enhancing the transparency and accountability of sports associations, establishing a sports ombudsman, and providing more financial incentives and career prospects for athletes. I hope that the government will continue to provide active support for sports development in respect of policy and resources, taking the overall development of sports in Hong Kong to new heights. This publication deeply examines the existing legislative framework and legal mechanisms for sports and also highlights the importance of sports law in Hong Kong.

I am honored to have the opportunity to write the preface for this pioneering book, which is the first of its kind to offer a very informative overview of sports law in Hong Kong. I would like to express my sincere gratitude to the authors, for their excellent work and dedication in producing this valuable reference for the sports community, the legal profession, and the general public. I hope that this book will serve as a useful and informative resource for anyone who is interested in learning more about sports law and the general development of sports in Hong Kong. I also hope that this book will inspire more dialogue, research, and collaboration among different stakeholders to further develop and improve the sports law landscape in Hong Kong. Together, we can make Hong Kong a leading sports city in the region and the world.

Hon Vincent CHENG Wing-shun, MH, JP
Legislative Council Member

In recent years, the development of sports in Hong Kong has entered an exciting new era. Since 2021, Hong Kong has achieved unprecedented results in various sports, excelling at events such as the Olympics, Paralympics, Asian Games, World Championships, and Asian Championships. These remarkable accomplishments have not only fostered strong social support for the development of elite sports but also underscored the importance of public health. Together, these factors signal the dawn of a transformative period for Hong Kong's sports industry.

Following the release of the Chief Executive's 2024 Policy Address, discussions have intensified regarding the overall strategy for the sports industry, including sports arbitration. Over the past three decades, the landscape of sports has evolved significantly, with each society possessing its own unique culture and background. In this context, the book *International Encyclopaedia of Laws: Sports Law* is a timely publication that can address emerging needs and provide cost-efficient solutions to sports-related disputes in the future, making it a valuable resource for the industry.

Forewords

In November 2024, the Sports Federation and Olympic Committee of Hong Kong, China submitted a Corporate Governance Review Report to the government. The report aims to instigate effective governance for sports associations in Hong Kong by enhancing their credibility, reliability, fairness, transparency, and accountability. Effective governance underpinned by a robust legal framework, will be instrumental in accelerating the development of the sports industry.

Over the past thirty years, Hong Kong has encountered various legal challenges in sports, such as injury claims, compensation, administrative disputes over athletes' prize money allocation, controversies surrounding the selection of elite athletes, and issues related to retirement and election mechanisms within the executive committees of sports associations.

More recently, several controversies have arisen within the sports community, including eligibility issues for representatives of the Hong Kong team, the use of government resources by sports associations, incidents involving the national anthem and flag, and the so-called Messi incident. We anticipate that, as the process of sports industrialization advances, new and complex legal challenges are likely to arise. These may include issues related to patents, image rights, trademark law, sponsorship contracts, venue and equipment management, labor rights, antitrust law, and employment law. To embrace this era of sports industrialization, it is imperative that we prepare for these challenges proactively; otherwise, we may risk losing our momentum of recent successes and missing pivotal opportunities to position Hong Kong as a leader in the global sports industry. Addressing the complexities of issues in the sports industry must involve legal concepts, frameworks, logic, and historical context. This book will significantly contribute to knowledge of sports law and serve as a foundation for resolving sports disputes.

Hong Kong Baptist University is set to offer its first undergraduate degree in sports industry management in 2025. This handbook will be an excellent reference for the sports law course under the new curriculum. By linking legal concepts, theories, and case studies to Hong Kong's sports history, it lays a solid foundation for the development of sports industry professionals in the region.

We are deeply monored to have the opportunity to write the preface for this pioneering publication, as it signifies an important milestone in the study of sports law in Hong Kong. This is a historic moment that marks a new era in Hong Kong's sports history and industry. We believe that this book will not only inspire meaningful discussions and the exchanges of ideas among various stakeholders in the sports profession but also provide much-needed support to sports administrators navigating through complex legal challenges and disputes.

Prof. Sandy SC Li
(Director of Wellness and Human Development, Hong Kong Baptist University)
Prof. Patrick WC Lau
(Chair of the Department of Sport, Physical Education and Health; Associate Director of Wellness and Human Development (Research), Hong Kong Baptist University)

Acknowledgment

We would like to give special thanks and recognition to **Mr. C.M. Chan**, Past President of The Law Society of Hong Kong, for his contribution to the sessions "Tax law applied to Sport", "Agents' Regulations", "Trade Unions" and "Sports Dispute Resolution", and **Mr. Bryan Chan** for his contribution to the sessions "Sports and Employment – Introduction", "Sources of Employment Law" and "Employment Relationship" in this book.

Acknowledgment

General Introduction

§1. General Background

1. The global sports industry is expected to achieve over 10% annual growth rate to grow to USD 680 billion by 2028.[1] The strong spirit of athletes of the Hong Kong Special Administrative Region of the People's Republic of China (HKSAR) in international competitions has been demonstrated through their high achievements. In 2022–2023, a total of 141 medals (including 25 gold medals) were won at the World Championships[2] and the Asian Championships. The 2024 Paris Olympics saw Hong Kong winning 4 medals, 2 of which were gold[3] The success of the Hong Kong Sevens, Standard Chartered Marathon, Hong Kong Open (badminton, golf, tennis) and other major sport events, has demonstrated that Hong Kong is capable of hosting mega sports events, and with the opening of Kai Tak Sports Park in 2025, Hong Kong could more fully participate in the national and global sports industry advancements, and at the same time advance the national initiative for 45% of the population to exercise regularly by 2035, to become a modern leading sports country by 2050.

2. Sports in Hong Kong have a profound impact on society, the community, and the economy. It is pertinent to acknowledge the historical role of sports in unifying the people of Hong Kong over the past century. For example, the 2000 Sydney Olympics was the first Olympic Games after Hong Kong's return to China. Just over a month after the Olympics concluded, twenty-five gold medalists from the national team came to Hong Kong for a series of performance events including badminton, table tennis, and diving. The gold medalists' visit to Hong Kong produced a city-wide sensation, featuring extensive performances and interactivity with Hong Kong residents. These interactions between national Olympic athletes and Hong Kong people reinforce the Chinese identity and sense of belonging in Hong Kong after 1997. Since then, Olympic medalists' delegation visits to Hong Kong after the Olympic Games have become a tradition (i.e., 2004 Athens Olympics, 2008 Beijing Olympics, 2012 London Olympics, 2016 Rio Olympics and 2020 Tokyo Olympics).

---

1. Gough, C. (2024) Global sports market revenue 2028.
2. "Our Focus: Excelling in Sports, International Result" (Hong Kong Sports Institute) https://www.hksi.org.hk/annual-report/2022-23/our-focus-excelling-in-sports/international-results/.
3. "Olympic Games Paris 2024: Complete list of Medal Winners from Hong Kong, China" (Olympic Paris, Aug. 1, 2024) https://olympics.com/en/news/olympic-games-paris-2024-hong-kong-medal-winners-full-list, accessed Sep. 23, 2024.

3. Hong Kong as a special administrative region of China has a diverse sports landscape combining Western sports (Baseball, Football, Horse Racing, Ice Hockey, Rugby, Tennis), Asian sports (Muay Thai, Kabaddi, Karate, Sepak Takraw, Taekwondo), and Chinese sports (Dragon Boat, GO, Lion Dance, Martial Arts, Shuttlecock) in Hong Kong.

4. During the late nineteenth century, resources were scarce in Hong Kong, resulting in limited development of sports within the city. However, with an increasing number of Chinese immigrants migrating to Hong Kong in the early twentieth century, residents were prompted to establish their own sporting clubs and participate in traditional British sports, such as rugby and cricket. To promote sports activities among Chinese residents, the Chinese Young Men's Christian Association was established in Hong Kong in 1901. This organization played a significant role in promoting the development of sports in Hong Kong, creating new sport clubs for cricket, tennis, and swimming.

5. Noteworthy is the establishment of sporting clubs such as the Hong Kong Jockey Club (HKJC) founded in 1884, the Hong Kong Football Club founded in 1886, the Hong Kong Cricket Club founded in 1851 and the Royal Hong Kong Yacht Club have laid the foundation for the success of the Hong Kong sports. Furthermore, the development of the socio-economic environment has led to the introduction of some modern sports such as Dodgebee, Electronic sports (Esports), Floor Curling, Formula E (The Hong Kong ePrix), Frisbee, Mixed Martial Art (MMA) and Pickleball.

6. In contrast to other sports, football has maintained a consistent level of popularity in Hong Kong since its introduction. The South China Athletic Club was established in 1910, eventually changing its name to the South China Athletic Association in 1922. This association played a pivotal role in promoting football and other sports in Hong Kong, which contributed immensely to their popularity in the city. While the development of sports was disrupted by the Second World War and the Korean War, the 1950s marked the beginning of a new phase of sports development in Hong Kong. In particular, the SF&OC was established in 1950. SF&OC played a crucial role in representing Hong Kong on the international stage as the official Olympic committee, thereby enabling Hong Kong to directly participate in the Olympic Games.

7. Despite the achievements of the SF&OC, sports development remained a peripheral concern for the government's policy agenda. However, this situation changed in the late 1960s when riots and protests broke out against the government, prompting them to reassess the social and cultural development of Hong Kong, including sports. Due to the rising public demand for sports in Hong Kong, the government set up the Council for Recreation Sport in 1973. This event is considered a defining moment in Hong Kong's sports history, as it signaled the government's ad hoc focus on sports. Elite sports started to garner more widespread attention with the establishment of the Jubilee Sports Centre (JSC) in 1982. Initially, the JSC gained recognition for its top-notch amenities, coaches, and administration, where its training center and venues were notably expansive. In 1991, the JSC expanded its mandate and underwent a transformation to become the HKSI. This re-envisioning positioned it as the preeminent center for elite sports training and research in Hong Kong. Hong Kong Sports Development Board (HKSDB) was established in 1990. Its role was to provide funding support to national sports associations, offer direct services of sport medicine, sports science, and sport training to elite athletes, and manage HKSI. HKSDB was dissolved in 2004 after the Sports Policy Review.

8. It is also vital to highlight the achievements and milestones in Hong Kong sports history, such as Lee Lai Shan—the first athlete to win the Olympic Gold Medal for Hong Kong as a professional windsurfer, Sarah Lee Wai-sze—with two bronze Olympic medals for cycling, Siobhan Bernadette Haughey—the first Hong Kong athlete to win two Olympic Silver and two Olympic Bronze medals in swimming in the 2020 Tokyo Olympics (although Tokyo Games was held in 2021, it is still named 2020 Tokyo Olympics under International Olympic Committee (IOC)) and 2024 Paris Olympics respectively, and Edgar Cheung Ka-long—winning two consecutive Olympic Gold medals in fencing (foil).

9. In order to encourage athletes, the HKJC provides cash incentives to athletes participating in major games and achieving top results through the three-year Jockey Club Athlete Incentive Awards Scheme (JCAIAS) up to 2025.[4] The games covered by the JCAIAS include the Olympic and Paralympic Games, Asian Games, Asian Para Games, World University Games, National Games and National Games for Persons with Disabilities as well as their respective winter Games.[5] The table below is the details of the JCAIAS cash incentives distributed to the athletes in the Paris 2024 Olympic Games which took place from July 26 to August 11, 2024:

	Individual	*Team*
Gold	HKD 6,000,000	HKD 12,000,000
Silver	HKD 3,000,000	HKD 6,000,000
Bronze	HKD 1,500,000	HKD 3,000,000
4th	HKD 750,000	HKD 1,500,000
5th–8th	HKD 375,000	HKD 750,000

10. Hong Kong is also the home of many mega sporting events. The Hong Kong Open is a major international golf tournament which was first held in 1959 and has been conducted consistently for over six decades at the Hong Kong Golf Club in

4. *Jockey Club raises cash incentives for Hong Kong, China athletes participating in the Paris Olympics,* The HKJC (July 2024), https://corporate.hkjc.com/corporate/corporate-news/english/2024-07/news_2024070902015.aspx.
5. *"JCAIAS,"* HKSI, https://www.hksi.org.hk/support-to-athletes/awards/hong-kong-jockey-club-athlete-incentive-awards-scheme/.

Fanling.[6] The Hong Kong Open 2023 was part of the International Series on the Asian Tour, where prizes were up to USD 2 million.[7] Similarly, the prestigious Hong Kong Rugby Sevens forms a core part of the World Rugby Sevens Series, with the first tournament being played in 1976 with twelve teams participating,[8] and quickly evolved into a renowned rugby sevens competition. The annual Hong Kong Standard Chartered Marathon is another large sporting event held in Hong Kong. It attracts thousands of runners globally to compete in a run across many landmarks in Hong Kong. In 2024, 74,000 people participated in the marathon with around fifty top international runners competing for the prize.[9] The Hong Kong Cyclothon and the International Dragon Boat Festival play pivotal roles in the development of sports in the region, fostering community engagement and promoting sports culture. Meanwhile, the International Dragon Boat Festival, celebrated for its rich cultural heritage, not only attracts international teams but also unites local communities in a vibrant display of teamwork and Chinese tradition. Together, these events stimulate interest in various sports, inspire grassroots initiatives, and contribute to Hong Kong's reputation as a hub for sporting excellence, ultimately cultivating a healthier and more active society.

11. In recent years, Hong Kong has continued to place further emphasis on developing its elite sports, especially in training athletes who can compete on an international scale. These aims were emphasized in the 2002 report entitled "Towards a More Sporting Future" published by the Sports Policy Review Team of the Home Affairs Bureau, which prompted the implementation of a three-pronged strategy for the long-term sports development in Hong Kong:[10]

a. developing a strong supporting culture in the community;
b. achieving greater excellence in sport by providing more support for elite athletes; and
c. raising Hong Kong's profile as a center for international sports events.

12. In response, the government has increased support for the sporting community by constructing new sporting facilities, such as the Hong Kong Velodrome in

---

6. *Dates Confirmed for Historic Hong Kong Open*, Asian Tour (2023) https://www.asiantour.com/blog/dates-confirmed-for-historic-hong-kong-open?id=ISHK%3Fseason%3D2024.
7. Ryan Ballengee, "2023 Hong Kong Open purse, winner's share, prize money payout" (GNN, November 2023), https://thegolfnewsnet.com/ryan_ballengee/2023/11/12/2023-hong-kong-open-purse-winners-share-prize-money-payout-130564/#:~:text=The%202023%20Hong%20Kong%20Open%20purse%20is%20set,to%20the%20Asian%20Tour%27s%20prize%20money%20distribution%20chart assessed on Sep. 25, 2024.
8. *About—The Hong Kong Sevens,* Hong Kong Sevens (2022) https://hksevens.com/about-us/the-hong-kong-sevens#:~:text=The%20first%20tournament%20was%20played,World%20Rugby%20Sevens%20Series%20calendar.
9. Llewellyn Cheung, "Hong Kong Marathon returns to pre-pandemic levels with 74,000 runners" South China Morning Post (January 2024), https://www.scmp.com/video/hong-kong/3249225/hong-kong-marathon-returns-pre-pandemic-levels-74000-runners. assessed on Sep. 24, 2024.
10. Panel on Home Affairs, Background brief prepared by the Legislative Council Secretariat for the meeting on Jun. 12, 2015, Sports Development in Hong Kong, https://www.legco.gov.hk/yr14-15/english/panels/ha/papers/ha20150612cb2-1637-4-e.pdf.

2013 and Kai Tak Sports Park in 2024. Funding has also been increased by several subventions over the years. In particular, the government has set up an Elite Training Grant and Sports Aid Grant for athletes under the Individual Athletes Support Scheme. Moreover, Hong Kong has played host to a range of international sporting events, including the 2024 Union Cycliste Internationale, the 2024 World Triathlon Cup, the Hong Kong Squash Open 2024, and the annual Standard Chartered Hong Kong Marathon.

13. Additionally, it is worth mentioning the Chief Executive's 2022 Policy Address, in which the Culture, Sports and Tourism Bureau (CSTB) announced a ten-year Development Blueprint for sports and recreation facilities to enhance professionalism in the sports sector and to support athletes with training and venue in their participation in major sports competitions worldwide. This comprehensive planning showcases Hong Kong's increasing focus on sports and marks the growth of further sporting events within the region.

14. In Hong Kong, the CSTB is responsible for the promotion and implementation of the government's three policy objectives of sports development, including promoting sports in the community, supporting elite sports and promoting Hong Kong as a center for major international sports events, enhancing professionalism and developing sports as an industry. The synergy between culture, sports and tourism is expected, consequently, sport industrialization will emerge in Hong Kong.

15. In February 2025, the Law Society of Hong Kong will be hosting a mega international sports law conference to explore and address the legal issues relating to sports and raise awareness of how to best shape the development and maintenance of the sports development scene.

16. In terms of legislation, Hong Kong is recognized as a region with non-interference in sports, as stated in Article 148 of the Hong Kong Basic Law:

> The relationship between non-governmental organizations in fields such as education, science, technology, culture, art, sports, the professions, medicine and health, labour, social welfare and social work as well as religious organizations in the Hong Kong Special Administrative Region and their counterparts on the mainland shall be based on the principles of non-subordination, non-interference and mutual respect.

17. Each sport in Hong Kong has its own governing body, such as Badminton Association of Hong Kong, China (HKBA) for Badminton, the Football Association of Hong Kong, China Limited (HKFA) for Football, Hong Kong China Rugby Union (HKRU) for Rugby, Cricket Hong Kong, and China for Cricket. This allows local sports associations to have a certain level of competency and promote the autonomy of sports. In terms of sports-related crimes such as match-fixing and game rigging, relevant departments such as Independent Commission Against Corruption (ICAC) and the Hong Kong Police Force are responsible for the investigation of the crime. With effective enforcement, Hong Kong's sporting events could continue its dedication to sports integrity and secure a rousing match for fans every time.

18. Sports also serve as a powerful tool for fostering connections and understanding between nations/regions, illustrating the enduring impact of sports in shaping global diplomacy. In the intricate realm of sports politics and foreign affairs, few events rival the significance of the historic Ping Pong Diplomacy between the United States and China in the early 1970s. This groundbreaking exchange, initiated during the World Table Tennis Championships in Nagoya, Japan, served as a catalyst for thawing decades of frosty relations between the two nations. Just as table tennis players bridged the divide between the U.S. and China through friendly competition, modern-day sports diplomacy continues to play a pivotal role in international relations, illustrating the enduring impact of sports in shaping global diplomacy such as the China Women's Volleyball Diplomacy after the five-time world and Olympic champions between 1981-1986, and Yao Ming Basketball Diplomacy.

§2. Sources of Sports Law

19. The statutory sports law in Hong Kong is part of the Basic Law of the HKSAR. Chapter VI of the Basic Law covers sports.

20. According to Article 143 of the Basic Law, the Government of Hong Kong may on its own formulate sports policies, and non-governmental sports organizations may continue to exist and develop in accordance with the law.

21. The duty/standard of care is also applicable to sports activities.[11]

22. It is important for individuals and organizations involved in sports in Hong Kong to be familiar with the related laws and regulations to ensure compliance and promote fair play and integrity in the sporting community.

§3. Specificity of Sports

23. The Hong Kong government has recognized the specificity of sports by heavily investing in sports facilities and infrastructure, as well as establishing a wide range of policies and initiatives to promote sports participation and development within the community. This includes various city-wide competitions hosted throughout the year such as the Hong Kong Games, Corporate Games and Masters Games, as well as educational schemes aimed at encouraging participation in sports among the younger generation, such as the Young Athletes Training Scheme and the School Sports Programme under the Leisure and Cultural Services Department (LCSD).

11. *Condon v. Basi* [1985] 2 All ER 453, 1 WLR 866.

24. Furthermore, the unique nature of sports has also been acknowledged by the then Secretary of Justice, Teresa Cheng Yeuk-wah, SC, at the Sports Dispute Resolution Conference under Hong Kong Legal Week 2020, who emphasized that the modern sports world is highly institutionalized, commercialized and regulated.[12] In particular, in order to promote the development of e-sports, the government has exempted e-sports venues from the license requirement under the Amusement Game Centres Ordinance (Cap. 435). This decision was underpinned by three principles: business facilitation, removing red tape and barriers, and ensuring the safety of premises.

25. Since the regulation of gambling in 1977, the government has authorized the lawfulness of betting on horse races and football matches under the Gambling Ordinance (Cap. 148) and Betting Duty Ordinance (Cap. 108), thus recognizing the commercialized aspect of the sport.

26. In addition, the government has also prioritized promoting equality in sports to foster social cohesion and community development. To this end, policies and programs have been implemented to provide equal opportunities for female athletes, disabled individuals and underprivileged children. These include the Hong Kong Women's Sevens, training programmes tailored-made to people with different types of disabilities, and the Community Sports Club Programme, which supports the establishment of sports clubs in local communities.

27. To facilitate the successful hosting of sporting events, sports associations in Hong Kong are empowered to set up and adopt guidelines governing the practice of sport and the organization of competitions with the aim of ensuring compliance with sports rules through a fair and just administrative system and disciplinary measures for resolving sporting violations. Certainly, sports rules must comply with fundamental human rights, the principles of public law and the laws of the region. Hong Kong has generally relied upon Public Law, Tort Law and various administrative guidelines set up by both the government and various sports associations to facilitate the development of sports within the region.

28. Lastly, the government has acknowledged the distinctive relationship between sports and tourism. In particular, the recent significant investment in the construction of the Kai Tak Sports Park could position Hong Kong as a prime location for hosting major international sporting events, attracting sports enthusiasts from around the globe to attend the city's sports events, thereby boosting tourism within the region.

---

12. Teresa Cheng Yeuk-wah, SC, Secretary for Justice, "Keynote Speech" Sports Dispute Resolution (Conference under the Hong Kong Legal Week 2020, Hong Kong, Nov. 5, 2020) https://www.info.gov.hk/gia/general/202011/05/P2020110500544.htm.

§4. Principles of Good Governance and Ethics in Sport

29. Sports is defined by the Oxford Dictionary as "[an] activity involving physical exertion and skill, esp. (particularly in modern use) one regulated by set rules or customs in which an individual or team competes against another or others. Frequently in plural."[13] This set of rules or customs differs between different types of sports, but one key fundamental commonality among all the sports played in the global arena is "ethics." To allow athletes to fairly compete and display their skills, there must be integrity among players to maintain the integrity of the sport. The standard of integrity will be set by custom and athletes and those administering the sport will need to comply with those standards to enable a fair playing field. Good governance among teams and among institutions is for all participating in those sports to be aware of the standard of integrity and ethical rules, to lend credibility to the sports results and achievements, and to enable proper, effective and large-scale development of sports.

30. The Hong Kong government has recognized the importance of such governance. For example, in January 2012, the Legislative Council Panel on Home Affairs issued a paper on Governance and Monitoring of and Funding of the National Sports Associations, to discuss the progress of improvement measures that have been introduced earlier.[14] In June 2023, the Legislative Council Panel on Home Affairs, Culture and Sports issued a paper on Sports Policy and Promoting Development of Sports in Hong Kong. To promote the development of sports development in Hong Kong, the government has significantly increased the recurrent resources dedicated to sports development from around HKD 5.2 billion in 2018-2019 to an estimated figure of HKD 7.4 billion in 2023-2024.[15]

31. It is *trite* that a major threat to the good governance, ethics and integrity of sports is bribery. To address this, in 2011, the ICAC launched the Best Practice Reference for National Sports Associations,[16] to remind NSAs to operate with a high degree of integrity, accountability and transparency. This best practice reference was prepared in consultation with the LCSD, the SF&OC and various sports associations, and it sets out recommended practical measures "for sports bodies to enhance

13. Oxford English Dictionary, sport, n.[1] meanings, etymology and more, https://www.oed.com/dictionary/sport_n1?tab=meaning_and_use&tl=true#21244919.
14. Legislative Council Panel on Home Affairs, Governance and Monitoring of and Funding for the National Sports Associations, https://www.legco.gov.hk/yr11-12/english/panels/ha/papers/ha0113cb2-772-3-e.pdf.
15. Legislative Council Panel on Home Affairs, Culture and Sports: Sports Policy and Promoting Development of Sports in Hong Kong, https://www.legco.gov.hk/yr2023/english/panels/ha/papers/ha20230612cb2-539-5-e.pdf.
16. Corruption Prevention Department, Best Practice Reference for Governance of National Sports Associations, https://www.hkbaseball.org/userfiles/file/Guides/ICAC_Governance_of_NSAs_eng.pdf.

governance, step up integrity management and devise a fair system to select athletes to represent Hong Kong in international competitions."[17]

32. Sports associations and institutes have also developed their own set of rules to encourage good governance and to set ethical standards.

33. Currently, the HKSI, which provides training to athletes and offers qualifications in sports training, has various policies, such as the Hong Kong Sports Institute Coaching Code of Ethical Conduct (HKSI CCEC)[18] and the Measures on the Promotion of Racial Equality.[19]

34. The HKSI CCEC sets out guidelines on tenets for coaches such as ethical principles, competence, integrity, professional responsibility, respect and dignity and concern for others' welfare. These guidelines include the need for coaches to, *inter alia*, ensure they have the relevant competence to handle the duties they undertake and deliver proper training, to maintain proper channels and mindsets for communication and to be honest, fair, and respectful of others, to be aware of and eliminate biases, and to consult with, refer to, or cooperate with other professionals and institutions to the extent needed to serve the best interest of their athletes.

35. However, the world of sports is rapidly changing and polices need to be adjusted to adapt and progress.

36. The government has also engaged a consultant to study the relevant issues and has consulted the business and sports sectors, to identify the opportunities and challenges in the development of sports professionalism and sports as an industry, and put forward recommendations across four key domains, including sports administration and strategy, grassroots sports and sports culture, growing the sports economy, and professionalization of the sports workforce.[20]

37. In the Chief Executive's 2024 Policy Address delivered on October 16, 2024, Chief Executive Mr. John KC Lee, GBM, SBS, PDSM, PMSM discussed the aim to enhance not only the mechanism of providing direct financial support for athletes and promotion of sports but also the governance reform of the NSAs, and the

---

17. *Governance guidelines issued to sports bodies*, news.gov.hk, Dec. 16, 2011, https://www.news.gov.hk/en/categories/law_order/html/2011/12/20111216_175906.shtml.
18. Hong Kong Sports Institute, Hong Kong Sports Institute Coaching Code of Ethical Conduct, https://www.hksi.org.hk/training-the-athletes/high-performance-coaching/hksi-coaching-code-of-ethics Sports Institute.
19. Hong Kong Sports Institute, Measures on the Promotion of Racial Equality, https://www.hksi.org.hk/hksi/measures-on-the-promotion-of-racial-equality.
20. Legislative Council Panel on Home Affairs, Culture and Sports: Sports Policy and Promoting Development of Sports in Hong Kong, https://www.legco.gov.hk/yr2023/english/panels/ha/papers/ha20230612cb2-539-5-e.pdf.

enhancement of professionalism and development of sports as an industry.[21] This would include the need to understand what issues can be improved to progress forward.

38. One of the measures that the government has highlighted in 2024 is for SF&OC to make recommendations to ensure the NSAs are operating effectively so that athletes (including athletes with disabilities) can realize their potential in a fair and professional environment.[22]

39. The SF&OC has undergone reviews of the operation and governance of seventy-seven member out of eighty-three member associations in six major areas, being board governance, integrity management, selection of athletes, management of coaches and umpires, administration of membership, and general administration,[23] and in November 2024, it released the Code of Governance to the member sports associations to improve the governance level and operational transparency covering mechanisms for athlete selection as well as qualification and registration of coaches and referees, and complaint handling procedures.[24] A total of 243 specific requirements are set out in the Code of Governance.

40. Member associations are given two years to implement the Code of Governance and the SF&OC will issue certificates to compliant member associations in 2027. Member associations who fail to receive such certification of compliance may face funding suspensions from the government.

41. We expect that there will be continuing recommendations made to enhance good governance to maintain the highest ethical standards in the sports industry.

---

21. The Chief Executive's 2024 Policy Address, https://www.policyaddress.gov.hk/2024/public/pdf/policy/policy-full_en.pdf.
22. Paragraph 136 of The Chief Executive's 2024 Policy Address, https://www.policyaddress.gov.hk/2024/public/pdf/policy/policy-full_en.pdf.
23. SF&OC, Corporate Governance Review Report, https://www.hkolympic.org/wp-content/uploads/2024/11/2024-11-20-Corporate-Governance-Review-Report.pdf
24. Hong Kong United Times, Code of governance released for sports association covering athlete selection and board tenure, Nov. 20, 2024, https://hkut.news/2024/11/20/code-of-governance-released-for-sports-association-covering-athlete-selection-and-board-tenure/.

Part I. The Legal Framework

§1. Brief Introduction to Hong Kong's Public Law

42. Hong Kong is a special administrative region of the People's Republic of China (PRC). It enjoys a unique "One country, Two systems" approach, whereby it is the only common law jurisdiction within the PRC.

43. This special arrangement stems from the Joint Declaration on the question of Hong Kong, which was signed between the Chinese and British Governments on December 19, 1984. The Joint Declaration sets out, among other things, the basic policies of the PRC regarding Hong Kong, including the principle of "One Country, Two Systems," so that Hong Kong can maintain its capitalist system and lifestyle for fifty years after the return of Hong Kong to China. Pursuant to the Joint Declaration, these basic policies were stipulated in the Basic Law of Hong Kong, which was adopted on April 4, 1990, by the Seventh National People's Congress (NPC) of the PRC.

44. The Basic Law of Hong Kong, a constitutional document of Hong Kong, was made effective as of July 1, 1997, when Hong Kong was returned to China. It enshrines not only the principle of "One Country, Two Systems" but also Hong Kong's high degree of autonomy and the right for Hong Kong people to administer Hong Kong. A clear set of rules are set out to protect the freedoms of Hong Kong people and provide a framework for governance and the development of Hong Kong.

45. Hong Kong courts have the jurisdiction to interpret the Basic Law and adjudicate cases relating to the provisions of the Basic Law. If the courts need to interpret the provisions of the Basic Law concerning affairs which are the responsibility of the Central People's Government, or concerning the relationship between the Central Authorities and Hong Kong, and if such interpretation will affect the judgments on the cases, the Hong Kong courts shall, before making their final judgments which are not appealable, seek an interpretation of the relevant provisions from the Standing Committee of the NPC.[25]

46. The power of amendment of the Basic Law shall be vested in the NPC.[26]

---

25. Article 158 of the Basic Law.
26. Article 159 of the Basic Law.

I. Sports in the Basic Law

47. The right to enjoy sports is a fundamental right and is expressly enshrined in the Basic Law. In fact, the word "sports" is mentioned over twenty times within the text, reflecting the importance of the government in ensuring that the rights to sports are ensured for the people of Hong Kong.

48. Specific provisions regarding the maintenance and development of Hong Kong's current systems and policies concerning key areas of public life are set out in Chapter VI "Education, Science, Culture, Sports, Religion, Labour and Social Services" of the Basic Law. Among other important aspects of public life such as education, science, culture, and religion, sports was listed as being of equal importance. The government recognizes that these aspects are important for social stability and development.

49. The development and promotion of public sports activities are aligned with the goal of improving the physical fitness levels of the general public. These are part of the state's objectives pursuant to the Constitution, which include other missions such as protecting the people's health through the development of medical and health care, developing modern medicine and traditional Chinese medicine, encouraging and supporting the running of various medical and health facilities by rural collective economic organizations, state enterprises, public institutions and neighborhood organizations, and promoting public health activities.

50. Pursuant to the high degree of autonomy that was granted to Hong Kong, Article 143 of the Basic Law under Chapter VI stipulates that the Hong Kong Government shall, on its own, formulate policies on sports. At the same time, non-governmental sports organizations may continue to exist and develop in accordance with the law.[27] This gives certainty to private sports organizations to continue their activities and indicates that new private sports organizations are also welcomed to grow in Hong Kong.

51. The relationship between non-governmental organizations in sports in Hong Kong and their counterparts on the mainland is based on the fundamental principles of non-subordination, non-interference and mutual respect. This is provided for in Article 148 of the Basic Law:

> The relationship between non-governmental organizations in fields such as education, science, technology, culture, art, sports, the professions, medicine and health, labour, social welfare and social work as well as religious organizations in the Hong Kong Special Administrative Region and their counterparts on the mainland shall be based on the principles of non-subordination, non-interference and mutual respect.[28]

---

27. Article 143 of the Basic Law.
28. Article 148 of the Basic Law.

52. To protect the certainty and continuity of employment in subvented private sports organizations (i.e., organizations established to produce and develop goods and services on behalf of the government), the Basic Law provides that Hong Kong shall maintain the policy practiced prior to the return of Hong Kong to China in respect of subventions for non-governmental organizations in fields such as sports.[29] Accordingly, such persons serving in subvented organizations in Hong Kong prior to the return of Hong Kong to China may remain in their employment in accordance with the previous system.

53. Since many subvented organizations receive substantial funding from the government, some of which may be recurrent in nature, subvented organizations must be accountable to both the government and the community. To properly apply resources for the good of the community and sustain public trust in bodies which receive public funds, the government had created a Guide to Corporation Governance for Subvented Organizations.[30] The guide stipulates that the subvented organizations should attain, and maintain, high standards of corporate governance,[31] and the board of each subvented organization is responsible for its activities and performance. Like the fiduciary duties owed by directors in any company incorporated in Hong Kong, each member of the board has important responsibilities to discharge their responsibilities with a serious, professional, committed and honest approach.

II. Importance of the Sports Industry Reflected in the Law

54. The importance of practicing sports is a country-level matter. Pursuant to Article 57 of the Constitution of the PRC, the NPC of the PRC is the highest state organ of power. Its permanent organ is the NPC Standing Committee.[32] The NPC and the NPC Standing Committee exercise the legislative power of the state.[33] The NPC decides on the successful candidates of the State Council.[34] Under Article 89 of the Constitution of the PRC, the State Council shall exercise various functions and powers on important matters including directing and managing education, science, culture, health, sports and family planning work.

55. Before the return of Hong Kong to China, the importance of sports was already enshrined in the Basic Law. This can be demonstrated by the involvement of the sports sector in the Hong Kong government and law-making procedures, as highlighted below.

---

29. Article 144 of the Basic Law.
30. *Guide to Corporate Governance for Subvented Organisations,* Social Welfare Department (June 2015), https://www.swd.gov.hk/storage/asset/section/594/en/guide_to_cg_for_so_2015.pdf, accessed Jul. 23, 2024.
31. *Ibid.*
32. Article 57 of the Constitution of the PRC.
33. Article 58 of the Constitution of the PRC.
34. Article 62 of the Constitution of the PRC.

56. As mentioned earlier, the Basic Law provides Hong Kong with a high degree of autonomy and empowers Hong Kong to exercise executive, legislative and independent judicial power, including that of final adjudication. An Election Committee, composed of 1,500 members, split into 300 members in each sector, is broadly representative and represents the overall interests of society.[35] It has the power to nominate and elect 40 members of the LegCo,[36] being the body that enacts, amends and repeals the laws of Hong Kong.[37]

57. The Election Committee is split into five sectors, being:

First Sector: Industrial, commercial and financial sectors
Second Sector: The professions
Third Sector: Grassroots, labor, religious and other sectors
Fourth Sector: LegCo members, representatives of district organizations and other organizations
Fifth Sector: HKSAR deputies to the NPC, HKSAR members of the National Committee of the Chinese People's Political Consultative Conference and representatives of Hong Kong members of relevant national organizations.[38]

58. Sports, performing arts, culture and publication fall into the second sector of the Election Committee. The subsector is allocated thirty seats within this sector.[39]

59. The Election Committee has significant powers. The Election Committee nominates and elects the Chief Executive in accordance with the Basic Law.[40] The Chief Executive of Hong Kong is the head of the HKSAR[41] and is responsible for various duties including the implementation of the Basic Law, signing bills and budgets passed by the LegCo, promulgating laws, making decisions on government policies and issuing executive orders.

60. Furthermore, there are twenty-eight functional constituencies for the election of members of the LegCo, one being the "Sports, performing arts, culture and publication."

61. Despite being an inseparable part of China, Hong Kong has the special right to send its own sports representative teams to international competitions. Pursuant to Article 151 of the Basic Law, Hong Kong can use the name "Hong Kong, China" to maintain and develop relations and conclude and implement agreements with foreign states and regions and relevant international organizations in the appropriate fields, including the sports fields.

35. Annex I of the Basic Law (Method for the Selection of the Chief Executive of the HKSAR).
36. Annex II of the Basic Law (Method for the Formation of the LegCo of the of the HKSAR).
37. Article 73 of the Basic Law.
38. Annex I of the Basic Law (Method for the Selection of the Chief Executive of the HKSAR).
39. *Ibid.*
40. Once elected, the Chief Executive shall be appointed by the Central People's Government.
41. Article 43 of the Basic Law.

62. The legislation of the country and the region both indicate unwavering support for the development of sports in Hong Kong. This is momentous since Hong Kong athletes are given a chance to compete in events together with teams from China while maintaining their own special identity in such competitions to recognize their training and efforts.

III. Right to Practice Sport

63. Pursuant to the rights under the Basic Law, people in Hong Kong have the right to practice sport and are encouraged to do so.

64. The government has established various departments to help promote the development of sports. For example, the CSTB established in July 2022 is charged with promoting the development of sports in Hong Kong. It has a "Sports & Recreation Branch" tasked with the promotion and implementation of the government's three policy objectives of sports development, namely, to promote sports in the community, support elite sports and promote Hong Kong as a center for major international sports events.

65. There are existing sports and recreation facilities such as indoor sports centers, sports grounds, tennis courts, basketball courts, football pitches, swimming pool complexes, beaches, holiday camps and water sports centers managed by the LCSD.

66. With the recent uptake in exercise and sports participation, the facilities are frequently overbooked. Therefore, the CSTB has been considering the need to increase and enhance sports and recreational facilities in Hong Kong.

67. The enhancements include a new Kai Tak Sports Park, which is set to be 28 hectares of land to provide sports facilities for the community and home-grown athletes, and enables major international competitions to be hosted.[42]

68. In the 2017 Hong Kong Policy Address, the government announced the "Five-Year Plan for Sports and Recreation Facilities" (the "**Five-Year Plan**") to launch twenty-six projects to develop, improve and create new sports and recreation facilities.[43] The aim of the Five-Year Plan was to meet the demands of the public for the use of these sports grounds and to garner greater sports participation in the community. This is a significant project with an investment amount of HKD 20 billion. As of April 2024, funding approval has been given for twenty-one projects, to, *inter alia,* build out heated swimming pools, football pitches, tennis courts, and

42. CSTB, *Kai Tak Sports Park*, https://www.cstb.gov.hk/en/policies/sports-and-recreation/kai-tak-sports-park.html, accessed Apr. 12, 2024.
43. CSTB, *Five-Year Plan for Sports and Recreational Facilities*, https://www.cstb.gov.hk/en/policies/sports-and-recreation/sports-policy/sports-and-recreation-facilities/five-year-plan.html#:~:text=In%20the%20Policy%20Address%20delivered,existing%20sports%20and%20recreation%20facilities, accessed Apr. 12, 2024.

basketball courts, for public use.[44] Other projects under the Five-Year-Plan are due to be implemented by the government as well, under the necessary projects such as conducting technical feasibility studies, etc.

Qualification to represent Hong Kong

69. Individual sports associations may also impose qualification rules on their own. There is a need however to strike a balance between the system and the protection of athletes' interests. Recently, a 9-year-old swimmer was initially denied the chance to join a local championship due to the qualification rules of the Hong Kong China Swimming Association, saying that the status of the swimmer's swimming club is too low.[45] The association has allowed the boy to join the competition after sparked criticism received about its qualification rules[46] and said "*In the future, if there are any swimmers from competition members who [meet the] qualifying times [requirements], they can submit a written application to our association. The executive committee will consider each case individually based on the same principles.*"

Changing Nationality

70. There may be instances where an athlete has multiple nationalities, and they must decide which country they wish to represent in a competition. If an athlete used to represent Country A but wishes to then represent Country B, can they do so?

71. Under by-law to Rule 41 of the Olympic Charter, which governs the Olympic Games, a competitor who is a national of two or more countries at the same time may represent either one of them, as he may elect. However, after having represented one country in the Olympic Games, in continental or regional games or in world or regional championships recognized by the relevant International Sports Federation (IFS), he may not represent another country unless he meets the specific conditions that apply to persons who have changed their nationality or acquired a new nationality. One of the conditions is that a minimum of three years must have elapsed since the athlete last represented their former country. This period may be reduced or even canceled, with the agreement of the National Olympic Committee (NOC) and IFS concerned, by the Executive Board of the IOC. The decision on whether to allow the change will be considered taking into account the circumstances of each case.

72. The requirement for changing nationality in Fédération Internationale de Football Association (FIFA) is more lenient. The FIFA eligibility rules have been

---

44. Provision of Sports and Recreation Facilities—CSTB (cstb.gov.hk) accessed on Jun. 28, 2024.
45. Michael Shum, Singer Alex Fong slams swimming association for "unfair system," The Standard (Jul. 8, 2024), https://www.thestandard.com.hk/section-news/section/4/264178/Singer-Alex-Fong-slams-swimming-association-for-'unfair-system'.
46. Irene Chan, Swimming body allows young swimmer to join championships, as ex-athlete Alex Fong urges change to qualification rules, Hong Kong Free Press, (Jul. 15, 2024) https://hongkongfp.com/2024/07/15/hong-kong-swimming-body-allows-young-swimmer-to-join-championships-as-ex-athlete-alex-fong-calls-for-change/.

updated in 2020. If an athlete, before the age of 21, has not played more than three matches at "A" international level in any kind of football for his/her current association, whether in an official competition or non-official competition, he/she may change the national team even if he/she has participated in official competitions for the first country, provided he/she was eligible to represent a second country at the time he/she first played for their first country.[47]

73. Apart from recruiting dual-nationals, naturalization (i.e., renunciation of original nationality) has allowed Hong Kong to include non-native-born athletes and help form a multi-ethnic team in sports matches.

IV. Personality Rights

A. Background on Personality Rights

74. Personality rights generally refer to the right to privacy (which is a right to keep one's personal information and private life private and out of the public domain) and publicity rights (which are rights protecting a person's appearance, name, image, voice or personal attributes against the unauthorized commercial use).

75. In Hong Kong, PDPO safeguards individual privacy in relation to personal data. During the drafting of the PDPO, references have been made to the Organization for Economic Co-operation and Development Privacy Guideline 1980 and the EU Directive. Given the General Data Protection Regulation (GDPR) represents a remarkable evolution of data protection law from the EU Directive, new provisions and enhanced privacy rights are yet to be found under the PDPO.[48]

76. In Hong Kong, the right to privacy is protected under the Basic Law and Hong Kong Bill of Rights Ordinance (Cap. 383). Hong Kong sports persons are afforded a wide range of protections, including but not limited to personal data privacy rights, and intellectual property rights. Laws and legal principles such as the tort of passing off, defamation, violation of advertising codes, and breach of confidence under contract law are also relevant in protecting the interests of different stakeholders in the sports world.

77. Under some circumstances, if there is unauthorized use of a sports person's image, it might arguably be considered a contravention of the PDPO. Whether there is indeed a contravention will rest on, *inter alia*, whether there was unauthorized collection and handling of personal data.

47. FIFA Commentary on the Rules Governing Eligibility to Play for Representative Teams (January 2021), https://digitalhub.fifa.com/m/ccab990abf45fcf6/original/ro8mje8vw98yp3rvfbmi-pdf.pdf.
48. "Data Privacy Law: EU General Data Protection Regulation (GDPR)" (Office of the Privacy Commissioner for Personal Data, Hong Kong), https://www.pcpd.org.hk/english/data_privacy_law/eu/eu.html.

78. Personal data is defined under section 2(1) of the PDPO as "any data relating directly or indirectly to a living individual, from which it is practicable for the identity of the individual to be directly or indirectly ascertained, and in a form in which access to or processing of the data is practicable."[49] The question would then be whether the image is considered personal data.

79. The *Eastweek v. Privacy Commissioner*[50] concerned a lady whose photo was taken by an *Eastweek* magazine photographer while she was walking in Central, a business district center in Hong Kong. Her photo was published in the *Eastweek* magazine, along with criticism of her fashion sense. The *Eastweek* magazine did not mention her name or place of work but only published her photograph. However, her friends, family members and colleagues recognized her from the photographs in the magazine, and she felt upset and ridiculed as a result of the publication. She then filed a complaint to the Privacy Commissioner, who initially decided that there was a breach of Date Protection Principle 1(2)(b) on the part of *Eastweek* in collecting the complainant's personal data by an unfair means. *Eastweek* applied for a judicial review of the Privacy Commissioner's decision, but its application was dismissed by the Court of First Instance. However, upon appeal to the Court of Appeal, Eastweek succeeded in obtaining an order for appeal. The Court of Appeal decided that the photograph was not considered personal data. However, Wong JA offered a dissenting view that a photograph should be considered personal data, since it depicts the complainant and satisfies the three requirements under the definition of personal data, being that it is a document (e.g., visual image), which relates directly or indirectly to a living individual, and whose identity could practically be ascertained.

80. The case may have come to different results if the image was of a person who was widely known to the public, such as a popular athlete. If the image (i.e., the data) relates directly to a living individual (being the renown athlete) and is in such a format that can enable viewers to readily identify that athlete, then that image will arguably constitute personal data.

81. If the image is considered personal data, then the relevant provisions of the PDPO relating to its collection, handling and storage must be complied with. The PDPO prohibits the use of personal data for any new purpose which is not or is unrelated to, the original purpose when collecting the data, save where the data subject's express and voluntary consent has been obtained. Further, a data user must obtain informed consent before using a data subject's personal data for direct marketing. If one collects personal data from data subjects directly, he should inform the data subjects of the purpose of using their data. For example, if an athlete returning from a competition greeted fans at the airport and had their photo taken by the media for reporting the return of the athlete, this would not, on its own, be deemed consent by the athlete to have that photo used for commercial endorsement of a health food product. If the image was used in that way, there would arguably have been a breach of the PDPO.

---

49. Section 2(1), *PDPO*.

50. *Eastweek Publisher Ltd & Anor v. Privacy Commissioner for Personal Data* (2000) 1 HKC 692.

82. There have been proposals to amend the PDPO. Included in those proposals[51] is the suggestion to expand the current definition of personal data to cover information relating to an "identifiable" natural person, so that it can more clearly cover image data.

83. If there are legal hurdles to utilizing the PDPO to protect the image rights, one can pursue a claim of tort of passing off. For passing off to be established, three elements are required: (1) goodwill, (2) misrepresentation, and (3) damage.[52]

84. In the case *Lau Tak Wah Andy v. Hang Seng Bank Ltd,*[53] Cantonese celebrity Andy Lau sued Hang Seng Bank for using his name, photograph, and likeness on credit cards and phone cards without his consent and applied for an injunction to prevent Hang Seng Bank from continuing use. The court decided that no misrepresentation was found and refused to grant the injunction. In its judgment, the court highlighted that a claim in the tort of passing off can only succeed if the defendant had passed off those items as items "promoted and/or endorsed by the plaintiff and/or as being marketed and promoted under a commercial arrangement with the plaintiff."[54]

85. In another passing-off case *Tam Wing Lun Alan v. Hang Mei Record,*[55] the court found that the defendant had engaged in passing off in its sale of cassette tapes which included covers of songs originally sung by Tam Wing Lun Alan. The Court found that all three elements of passing off have been established and awarded damages to the plaintiff. The court also cited an English case of *Draper v. Trist,*[56] setting out that "the true basis of the action is that the passing-off by the defendant of his goods as the goods of the plaintiff injures the right of property in the plaintiff, that right of property being his right to the goodwill of his business. The law assumes or presumes that, if the goodwill of a man's business has been interfered with by the passing-off of goods, damage results therefrom."[57]

86. Applying the findings from those cases, if any sports persons find that their image, name, or likeness are being used without their authorization, depending on the factual matrix, they may be able to protect themselves pursuant to provisions under the PDPO or pursuant to a claim for passing-off.

---

51. Legislative Council Panel on Constitutional Affairs, Review of the Personal Data (Privacy) Ordinance https://www.legco.gov.hk/yr19-20/english/panels/ca/papers/ca20200120cb2-512-3-e.pdf.
52. *Reckitt & Coleman Products Ltd v. Borden Inc* (No. 3) (1990) 1 W.L.R. 491.
53. *Lau Tak Wah Andy v. Hang Seng Bank Ltd* (2000) 1 HKC 280.
54. *Ibid.*, [4].
55. *Tam Wing Lun Alan & ORS v. Tam Kwok Hung T/A Hang Mei Record Co & Anor* (1991) 2 HKC 384.
56. *Draper v. Trist (1939)* 3 All ER 513.
57. *Ibid.*, p. 526.

B. Right of Erasure

87. The right of erasure is a right originating from the GDPR of the EU.[58] This right is also known as the "right to be forgotten" since it allows a person to request that their personal data be removed from certain records, or in other words, "erased."

88. However, this is not an unconditional right. Exercise of this right is subject to certain limitations. Under the GDPR, individuals may only succeed in exercising this right if:

a. the personal data is no longer necessary for the purpose originally collected or processed;
b. consent is the lawful basis for holding the data, and the individual withdraws their consent;
c. legitimate interests are the basis for processing, the individual objects to the processing of their data, and there is no overriding legitimate interest to continue this processing;
d. the personal data is being processed for direct marketing purposes and the individual objects to that processing;
e. the personal data is processed unlawfully;
f. it is to comply with a legal obligation; or
g. the personal data is processed to offer information society services to a child.[59]

89. In the EU, the right of erasure will not apply if the personal data is necessary for exercising the right of freedom of expression and information, or is in the interest of the public.[60]

90. In other words, for the sports industry, if an individual's personal data is used in a way that does not contradict the rights of freedom of expression or information, and the use is not related to the public interest, the individual may be able to exercise their right of erasure in the EU. They may have grounds to request that their personal data be removed. Where the personal information relates to matters of public interest, or matters that are within the reasonable rights afforded by the freedom of expression or information, the right of erasure will not apply. Examples specific to the sports industry are quite limited, but their application remains to be seen.

91. There is no right of erasure in Hong Kong.

---

58. Article 17 of the GDPR.
59. Information Commissioner's Office, *Right to erasure*, https://ico.org.uk/for-organisations/uk-gdpr-guidance-and-resources/individual-rights/individual-rights/right-to-erasure/#ib6, accessed on Apr. 16, 2024.
60. Regulation (EU) 2016/679 of the European Parliament and of the Council of Apr. 27, 2016, on the protection of neutral persons with regard to the processing of personal data and on the free movement of such data, and repealing Directive 95/46/EC (General Data Protection Regulation) Art. 17.

92. Instead, the PDPO provides that a data user must take all practicable steps to erase personal data held by the data user where the data is no longer required for the purpose.

93. With the developments in privacy laws worldwide, the PCPD has indicated that it "will keep abreast of the global personal data privacy development, and assess whether there is a pressing need for any reform in personal data law with a view to striking the proper balance between data privacy protection and other rights and interests, including the free flow of information, freedom of expression and of the press."[61]

94. On January 20, 2020, the Constitutional and Mainland Affairs Bureau released a consultation paper for discussion at the LegCo Panel on Constitutional Affairs meeting (Consultation Paper). The Consultation Paper proposed six amendments to the PDPO, including: (1) mandatory data breach notification mechanism; (2) data retention period; (3) sanctioning powers; (4) regulation of data processors; (5) definition of personal data; and (6) regulation of disclosure of personal data of other subjects.[62]

95. Regarding the definition of personal data, the PDPO currently only includes information that pertains to an "identified" person as personal data. However, considering the extensive use of advanced tracking and data analytics technology, the Consultation Paper proposed to expand the definition to include information related to an "identifiable" natural person. It is also consistent with the definitions adopted by some other jurisdictions.

96. Following the review of the PDPO in the Consultation Paper, the Personal Data (Privacy) (Amendment) Ordinance Bill 2021 was passed on September 29, 2021, and enacted on October 8, 2021. The amendment aims to combat doxing acts by criminalizing the intrusion of personal data privacy and granting the PCPD the statutory power to issue cessation notices demanding the termination of the disclosure of doxxing content. The rest of the amendments in the Consultation Paper have not been adopted yet.

97. A Panel on Constitutional Affairs meeting held on February 19, 2024, further reinforced that the PCPD, in conjunction with the government, was examining further amendments to the PDPO for the purposes of enhancing personal data protection and addressing the challenges presented by, *inter alia*, cyber technology.[63] The PCPD elaborated that current legislative amendment efforts are directed toward

---

61. PCPD Responses to Media Enquiry on The Right to be Forgotten (Feb. 8, 2018), https://www.pcpd.org.hk/english/news_events/media_enquiry/enquiry_20180208.html, accessed on Apr. 18, 2024.
62. *Review of the PDPO.* LC Paper No. CB(2)512/19-20(03). https://www.legco.gov.hk/yr19-20/english/panels/ca/papers/ca20200120cb2-512-3-e.pdf.
63. Paper provided by the Office of the Privacy Commissioner for Personal Data. LC Paper No. CB(2)157/2024(02) https://www.legco.gov.hk/yr2024/english/panels/ca/papers/ca20240219cb2-157-2-e.pdf.

establishing a mechanism for mandatory data breach notifications, requiring users of data to construct a data retention period policy, authorizing the PCPD to impose administrative fines, and direct regulation of data processors.[64]

98. Parties handling, using or storing personal data should also be aware of extraterritorial laws that may apply. For instance, the application of the PIPL of the PRC extends beyond territorial borders.

99. The PIPL specifies that the processing of personal information must adhere to principles such as legality,[65] fairness,[66] integrity,[67] necessity,[68] openness,[69] and transparency[70] and the purposes of processing personal information should be explicit and reasonable.[71] Organizations established or operating outside the PRC that intend to offer products or services, or analyze the data of individuals residing or located in the PRC must adhere to the provisions of the PIPL. Such organizations must also establish designated agencies or assign delegates to the PRC upon the processing of personal information of any individual within the territory of the PRC.[72]

100. Another set of extraterritorial laws to consider is the GDPR of the EU. Pursuant to Article 24 of the GDPR, the controller shall implement appropriate technical and organizational measures to ensure and to be able to demonstrate that processing is performed in accordance with this regulation. Furthermore, The GDPR applies when personal data is processed in relation to the activities of a controller in the EU, regardless of the location of the processing.[73] Therefore, organizations or companies, including those in Hong Kong, may be obligated to comply with the GDPR under specific circumstances such as when they monitor the behavior of individuals located within the EU or offer goods or services to EU residents.

§2. Governmental Conditions and Permits (Quotas, Work Restrictions)

101. The Government of Hong Kong has not implemented any flexible and fast-track visa policy for foreigners participating in cultural, art and sports activities in Hong Kong. Moreover, there are no specific guidelines on the circumstances under

---

64. *Background brief on the work of the Office of the PCPD.* LC Paper No. CB(2)157/2024(03) ca20 240219cb2-157-3-e.pdf (legco.gov.hk).
65. Article 10, PIPL.
66. Article 24, PIPL.
67. Article 5, PIPL.
68. *Ibid.*
69. Article 7, PIPL.
70. *Ibid.*
71. Article 6, PIPL.
72. Article 53, PIPL.
73. Article 3 GDPR.

which such overseas participants in cultural, art and sports activities need simpler visitor visas or more demanding employment visas.[74]

102. The Immigration Department states that it cannot offer a generalized policy or guideline, reiterating that it would consider many factors (e.g., nature of the activities, with or without employment, service contracts and remuneration) on a case-by-case basis. Some overseas cultural, art and sports activities participants may choose to enter into Hong Kong through a visitor visa instead.[75]

103. In the U.K., overseas amateurs can take part in non-work sports or entertaining activities through a visitor visa. Even experts invited by local organizations can also enter the country with a visitor visa for creative and sports activities for up to a month. For longer employment, foreign sportspersons and creative workers should file applications for an International Sportsperson visa. Applicants for the visa usually receive results within three weeks outside the U.K. or eight weeks inside the U.K.

104. The HKSI defines a full-time training athlete as an individual (for an able-bodied athlete) who receives a minimum of five days and twenty-five hours of supervised training per week.

105. No special condition or permit is needed for sport associations.

106. Unincorporated associations in Hong Kong are governed by the Societies Ordinance (Cap. 151). They are not separate legal entities. All unincorporated clubs or associations of persons are required to make a notification to the Societies Officer under the Societies Ordinance.

107. As a consequence of the lack of separate legal personality, each member of an unincorporated association will usually be liable jointly with other members for any liability the association may incur as a result of the act of its members, employees or agents.

108. Incorporated bodies are, however, governed by the Companies Ordinance (Cap. 622), and enjoy a separate legal personality.

109. Each company must comply with the filing obligations under the Companies Ordinance, otherwise, the responsible persons may be subject to a fine or imprisonment.

74. *Visa Requirement for Overseas Participants in Cultural, Arts and Sports Activities in Selected Places,* Research Office, LegCo Secretariat, (Dec 14, 2018), https://www.legco.gov.hk/research-publications/english/1819rt02-visa-requirement-for-overseas-participants-in-cultural-arts-and-sports-activities-in-selected-places-20181214-e.pdf.

75. *Ibid.*

110. Liability of members of a limited company is limited by the Articles of Association to the amount that the members respectively undertake to contribute to the assets of the company in the event of it being wound up.[76]

111. Where other Asian countries such as Qatar offer "mission passports" to foreign-born athletes which allows them to play for Qatar on temporary documents and remain citizens of their country of origin[77] or in other cases links of birth or cultural affinity, Hong Kong does not possess a fast-track mechanism in place for its foreign athletic talent to represent the region. Instead, naturalization to Hong Kong first requires a seven-year residency. This entitles athletes to permanent residency and basic citizenship rights and does not require them to give up their original nationality.[78]

112. According to a government press release,[79] at present, non-local people mainly apply for employment visas under the General Employment Policy (GEP) or the Admission Scheme for Mainland Talents and Professionals for coming to Hong Kong to participate in cultural, art and sports activities.[80] The government also launched the Immigration Facilitation Scheme on June 1, 2024, to provide immigration facilitation for visitors participating in short-term activities in designated sectors including sports.

113. Although it is a short-term solution and permit only, eligible non-local talent under the Immigration Facilitation Scheme may participate in the designated short-term activities for a period of up to fourteen consecutive calendar days upon each arrival, and be allowed to receive remuneration for the specified activities concerned.

§3. Tax Law Applied to Sport

I. No Separate Tax Regime for Sports in Hong Kong

114. There is no separate legal and tax regime to govern sports activities in Hong Kong. Sports activities are carried out by entities like any other business activities and are taxed accordingly. Generally speaking, sports activities can be conducted by

76. Companies Ordinance (Cap. 622), s. 8.
77. Jaafar Alloul and Laavanya Kathiravelu, "Constructing Qatari Citizenship in the shadow of the World Club" (Middle East Research and Information Project, 2022), https://merip.org/2022/11/constructing-qatari-citizenship-in-the-shadow-of-the-world-cup/#:~:text=The%20so%2Dcalled%20.
78. Sheung Ching Yung, David R Phillips, and Annie Hau Nung Chan, Athletic naturalization, nationality and nationalism—Naturalized players in Hong Kong's representative (national) football team, International Review for the Sociology of Sport 56, No. 6 (2021).
79. The Government of the Hong Kong SAR, "Immigration Arrangement for Non-local Individuals of Cultural, Arts and Sports Sectors," Press Release, Feb. 27, 2019, accessed Mar. 1, 2024, available at https://www.info.gov.hk/gia/general/201902/27/P2019022700571.htm.
80. *Ibid.*

limited liability companies, partnerships, or societies. LCSD of the Hong Kong Government maintains a list of NSAs and sports organizations in Hong Kong.[81]

115. General revenue law applies to the sports industry in Hong Kong and therefore, residents and non-residents are taxed in almost exactly the same way.

116. In Hong Kong, charitable institutions and trusts of a public character may be granted tax exemption under section 88 of the IRO (Cap. 112). Unless sports activities are carried out by organizations that are exempted from taxes under section 88 of the IRO, profits generated therefrom are subject to normal taxation.[82]

II. Hong Kong Tax System

General

117. Hong Kong has a simple and low tax system which is enshrined in the Basic Law, Hong Kong's constitutional document. There are only three direct taxes in Hong Kong: Profits Tax, Salaries Tax and Property Tax. Hong Kong does not impose capital gains tax, dividend tax or sales tax. The Inland Revenue Department (IRD; headed by the Commissioner of Inland Revenue) is tasked with the duty to collect revenue and enforce Hong Kong's tax system.

118. The main governing tax legislation in Hong Kong is known as the IRO (Cap. 112)[83]and its subsidiary legislation is the Inland Revenue Rules (Cap. 112A). Furthermore, where applicable, stamp duty is imposed under the Stamp Duty Ordinance (Cap 117).[84] In Hong Kong, stamp duty must be paid when certain documents are involved in buying or selling property or leasing property, or when Hong Kong stocks are bought or sold.

119. Hong Kong adopts a territorial approach to tax, i.e., it does not levy global tax; only profits arising in or derived from Hong Kong are taxable. For the sports industry, profits derived from international operations outside of Hong Kong are generally not subject to profits tax in Hong Kong.

120. According to the IRO, three income taxes are levied in Hong Kong, namely salaries tax, profits tax and property tax.

---

81. List of National Sports Associations and Sports Organizations in Hong Kong https://www.lcsd.gov.hk/en/.
82. IRO (Cap. 112) https://www.elegislation.gov.hk/checkconfig/success.jsp; Companies Ordinance (Cap. 622) https://www.elegislation.gov.hk/hk/cap622?m=0&pm=1&pmc=0; Societies Ordinance (Cap. 151) https://www.elegislation.gov.hk/hk/cap151?m=0&pm=1&pmc=0; Partnership Ordinance (Cap. 38) https://www.elegislation.gov.hk/hk/cap38?m=0&pm=1&pmc=0.
83. *Ibid.*
84. *Ibid.*

121. Profits Tax is levied on individuals, corporations, bodies of persons and partnerships, in respect of assessable profits arising in or derived from Hong Kong. The profits tax rate for the first HKD 2 million of assessable profits is 8.25% for corporations and 7.5% for unincorporated businesses. Profits above that amount are subject to the tax rate of 16.5% and 15%, respectively.

122. Salaries Tax is charged on all income from any office or employment and person arising in or derived from Hong Kong. The total maximum amount of tax payable is restricted to the standard rate (currently 15% or 16%) on the net total income of the individual concerned. Starting from the year of assessment 2024/25, for taxpayers whose net income exceeds Hong Kong Dollars HKD 5 million, the first HKD 5 million will be taxed at the rate of 15%, while the excess will be taxed at the rate of 16%.

123. Property Tax is charged to property owners which is levied at the standard rate (currently at 15%) in respect of the net assessable value of the property.

124. In addition, Ad Valorem stamp duty is computed at the applicable rate on the consideration or value of the property (ranging from HKD 100 to 8.5% of the consideration depending on the value and timing of the transactions). Stamp duty on the sale or purchase of any Hong Kong stock is also charged at rates which vary with the amount or value of the consideration.[85]

125. Profits tax, salaries tax, property tax and stamp duty are assessed separately. A permanent or temporary Hong Kong resident individual may elect to be assessed under personal assessment on the aggregate of their income or losses from all sources.[86]

Basic Information

126. The tax authority in Hong Kong is the IRD,[87] which administers the IRO (Cap. 112) and the Stamp Duty Ordinance (Cap. 117). The tax year runs from April 1 to March 31, and taxpayers are required to file their tax returns within one month of the date of issue. Hong Kong has different types of taxes, such as profits tax, salaries tax, property tax and stamp duty, which are assessed separately. Individuals can choose to be assessed under personal assessment, which allows them to combine their income or losses from all sources and claim additional allowances and deductions.

85. Stamp Duty Ordinance, Cap. 117 Laws of Hong Kong https://www.gov.hk/en/residents/taxes/stamp/stamp_duty_rates.htm.

86. For the latest Salaries Tax and Profits Tax rates, *see* IRD website at https://www.gov.hk/en/residents/taxes/taxfiling/taxrates/salariesrates.htm.

87. IRD Website: www.ird.gov.hk.

III. Salaries Tax

127. Salaries tax is levied on net chargeable income (assessable income less personal deductions and allowances) at progressive rates ranging from 2% to 17%, or at a flat rate (maximum rate) of 16% on assessable income less personal deductions, whichever calculation produces the lower tax liability. Salaries tax imposed on individuals applies on a sliding scale with a maximum rate that does not exceed 16% tax.

128. Under section 8 of the IRO, individuals earning income that arises in, or is derived from, a Hong Kong office or Hong Kong employment, or from services rendered in Hong Kong during visits of more than sixty days in any tax year, are subject to salaries tax. Since Hong Kong adopts a territorial basis of taxation; the notion of tax residency is largely irrelevant in assessing tax liability, except in a few specific situations.

129. Taxable "income from any office or employment" includes all forms of income and perquisites from an employer. It includes all cash emoluments, including bonuses and gratuities, "holiday benefits" and "rental value" in respect of a place of residence provided rent-free by the employer (which is commonplace for overseas sportspersons in Hong Kong).

130. In general, the nationality of the taxpayers has no bearing on tax liability. The test is whether income is considered to be "arising in or derived from Hong Kong" under section 8 of the IRO.

131. Except for directors' fees, a specific statutory exemption applies if an employee renders all of their services outside Hong Kong, or if an employee renders services in Hong Kong during visits to Hong Kong not exceeding a total of sixty days in a year of assessment. Conversely, if a non-resident engaged in non-Hong Kong employment renders services in Hong Kong during visits totaling more than sixty days in a year of assessment, they will be taxed on a pro-rata basis.

132. The provision of accommodation by an employer creates a taxable benefit equal to an amount ranging from 4% to 10% of the employee's other taxable income, depending on the type of accommodation. An employee is subject to salaries tax if their employment income is sourced in Hong Kong, even if they are not usually resident in the territory.

IV. Taxation of Non-resident Entertainers and Sportspersons in Hong Kong

133. Insofar as the basic charge to Salaries Tax is concerned, Hong Kong residents and non-Hong Kong residents (including sportsmen) are taxed in almost exactly the same way. Personal allowances are the same. For residents and non-residents, allowances are granted for spouse and children residing overseas. Obligations as to notification of chargeability to tax and tax clearance on departure from

Hong Kong are the same. The same criteria apply as regards whether the employee has a Hong Kong employment or a non-Hong Kong employment.

134. For a PRC resident who satisfies the "Present for not exceeding 183 days" exemption condition, he may be exempted from payment of salaries tax if he also satisfies the other two conditions as laid down in Article 14 of "The Arrangement between the Mainland of China and the Hong Kong for the Avoidance of Double Taxation and the Prevention of Fiscal Evasion with respect to Taxes on Income."

135. Under the IRO, tax must be withheld for fees due to a non-Hong Kong resident entertainer or sportsman. This fee withholding requirement applies to entertainment or sports performance in Hong Kong. The withholding tax rate varies depending upon whether the Hong Kong promoter or sponsor entered into an agreement directly with the non-Hong Kong resident entertainer or sportsman; or if the agreement was made with a non-Hong Kong resident agent, i.e., the representative of a non-Hong Kong resident entertainer or sportsman.

136. For agreements that are made directly with a non-Hong Kong resident entertainer or sportsman, a withholding tax rate of 10% will apply. For agreements that are made with a non-Hong Kong resident agent, a withholding tax rate of 10% will apply if the non-Hong Kong resident agent is an individual or partnership. A withholding tax rate of 11% will apply if the non-Hong Kong resident agent is a company. It should be noted that Hong Kong has concluded tax treaties with more than thirty countries in order to avoid double-taxation of income by both Hong Kong IRD and the Revenue authorities of other jurisdictions. Every tax treaty will specify the conditions for withholding tax between Hong Kong and the treaty country.[88]

V. Royalties Paid to Non-resident

137. No withholding taxes are levied in Hong Kong on dividends or interest paid to non-Hong Kong residents. However, royalties paid to non-resident individuals for the use of intellectual property rights in Hong Kong are deemed to arise from a Hong Kong business and are subject to an effective withholding tax rate of 2.25% (for the first HKD 2 million of royalty income) and 4.5% (for the remaining royalty income), if the individuals have elected to be subject to the two-tiered profits tax rates regime. The withholding tax rate is increased to 7.5% and 15% if the recipient is related to the payer, and if the intellectual property rights for which the royalties

88. For details, please refer to IRD Hong Kong Double Tax Treaties Guide, IRD Leaflet PAM 48(e) April 2024: Taxation of non-resident entertainers and sportsmen in Hong Kong and leaflet PAM 42 (e) "A guide to Salaries Tax for people coming to work in Hong Kong" for further information. IRD Leaflet PAM 48(e) April 2024: Taxation of non-resident entertainers and sportsmen in Hong Kong https://www.ird.gov.hk/eng/pdf/pam48e.pdf; DTAs https://www.ird.gov.hk/eng/tax/dta_cdta.htm; A Guide to Salaries Tax for people coming to work in Hong Kong https://www.ird.gov.hk/eng/pdf/pam42e.pdf.

are paid were previously owned by a person carrying on a profession, trade, or business in Hong Kong (subject to the application of the two-tiered profits tax regime). Such withholding tax on royalties paid to non-Hong Kong residents may be applicable to royalties paid in relation to sports activities.[89]

VI. Profits Tax

138. Profits Tax is charged under a two-tiered tax rates regime: companies and unincorporated businesses are subject to profits tax of no more than 16.5% and 15%, respectively (two-tiered corporate tax rate for companies and unincorporated businesses 8.25% and 7.25% respectively for the first Hong Kong Dollars HKD 2 million of profits, and 16.5% and 15% and for profits above that).

139. Anyone carrying on a profession, trade or business in Hong Kong is subject to profits tax on income arising in or derived from Hong Kong from that profession, trade or business. Taxable income is determined in accordance with generally accepted accounting principles. Business losses of an individual are calculated in the same manner as profits and may be carried forward indefinitely against future income in the same business or may be offset against the individual's other sources of income under personal assessment. In both cases, losses cannot be carried back. If an individual receives rental income but the rental activities do not constitute a business, the income is subject to property tax rather than profits tax.

Basic principles for determining the source of profits

140. The IRD issued "A Simple Guide on The Territorial Source Principle of Taxation"[90] in 2011 setting out Hong Kong's territorial source principle of taxation in that only profits which have a source in Hong Kong are taxable. Profits sourced elsewhere are not subject to Hong Kong Profits Tax. The Simple Guide gives a brief explanation, from the IRD's viewpoint, of how the principle operates and provides simple examples for illustrative purposes of the tests applied to different types of businesses.

> According to the Simple Guide, the subject of the source of profits has been decided in a number of court cases with the principles cited from the Simple Guide as follows:
>
> "(1) Matter of fact
> Whether profits arise in or are derived from Hong Kong depends on the nature of the profits and of the transactions which give rise to such profits.
>
> (2) Operations test
> The broad guiding principle is that one looks to see what the taxpayer has done to earn the profits in question and where he has done it. The

89. Please *see* Royalties in Part V for more details.
90. https://www.ird.gov.hk/eng/paf/bus_pft_tsp.htm.

proper approach is to identify the operations which produced the relevant profits and ascertain where those operations took place. The source of profits must be attributed to the operations of the taxpayer which produce them and not to the operations of other members of the taxpayer's group.

(3) Antecedent or incidental activities
The relevant operations do not comprise the whole of the taxpayer's activities. The focus is on establishing the geographical location of the taxpayer's profit-producing transactions as distinct from activities antecedent or incidental to those transactions.

(4) Place where decision is made
The place where the day-to-day investment/business decisions take place is only one factor which has to be taken into account in determining the source of profits. It is not usually the deciding factor.

(5) Gross profits from transactions
The distinction between Hong Kong profits and offshore profits is made by reference to the gross profits arising from individual transactions.

(6) Business presence overseas
A business may maintain a presence overseas which earns profits outside Hong Kong, but the absence of a business presence overseas does not, of itself, mean that all the profits of a Hong Kong business invariably arise in or are derived from Hong Kong. However, in the vast majority of cases where the principal place of business is located in Hong Kong and there is no business presence overseas, profits earned by that business are likely to be chargeable to Profits Tax in Hong Kong."[91]

Profits of trading firms (including entities in the sports industry)

141. In determining profits, the IRD will take into account the following factors:

(1) Contracts for purchase and sale
The factor that determines the locality of profits from trading in goods and commodities is generally the place where the contracts for purchase and sale are effected. "Effected" does not only mean that the contracts are legally executed but also covers the negotiation, conclusion and execution of the terms of the contracts. Following the Court of Appeal judgment (*Magna Industrial Co. Ltd v. CIR*),[92] it is now clear that a wider approach is necessary. The proper way is to look at all the relevant operations carried out to earn the profits, not simply the purchase and sale of the goods.[93]

(2) How relevant facts are considered

91. https://www.ird.gov.hk/eng/paf/bus_pft_tsp.htm.
92. *Magna Industrial Co Ltd v. Commissioner of Inland Revenue* [1997] HKLRD 173.
93. "Tax Free Profits of Hong Kong Trading firms" Global CPA, https://cpachina.com.hk/celebrity-news/160-tax-efficiency-of-international-trading-firms.

In considering the relevant facts the nature and quality of the activities matter more than their quantity. It is the cause and effect of such activities on the profits that is the deciding factor.

(3) Irrelevant facts
IRD will not take into account facts not directly related to the trading activities in determining the locality of profits such as renting office premises, recruiting general staff, or setting up office.

IRD's general practice

142. The IRD will look at whether the contracts of purchase and sale are effected in Hong Kong, if so, the profits are taxable here. If the contracts of purchase and sale are effected outside Hong Kong, the profits are not taxable in Hong Kong. Where either the contract of purchase or the contract of sale is effected in Hong Kong, the initial presumption is that the profits are taxable here. However, other relevant facts will have to be examined to determine the source of profits. Where the sale is made to a Hong Kong customer, the contract of sale will usually be taken as having been effected in Hong Kong. Where the effecting of the purchase and sale contracts does not require traveling outside Hong Kong but is carried out in Hong Kong by use of telephone, or other electronic means including the Internet, the contracts will be considered having been effected in Hong Kong. Trading profits are regarded as being either wholly taxable or wholly non-taxable here. Apportionment is generally not appropriate.

Advance rulings

143. To provide certainty in the operation of the territorial source principle, the IRD may provide "advance rulings" on the source of profits of a business for Profits Tax purposes. The service is subject to the payment of a fee.[94]

VII. Property Tax

144. Under section 5 of the IRO, property tax is charged to the owners of land and/or buildings in Hong Kong and is computed at the standard rate on the net assessable value of the property. The net assessable value is the assessable value after deduction of rates agreed to be paid and paid by the owner, less a 20% statutory allowance for repairs and outgoings.

VIII. Double Tax Treaty

145. As seen above, professional sportspersons who are non-residents in Hong Kong and derive income in Hong Kong can be taxed on their income produced in Hong Kong unless the sportsperson's home jurisdiction has entered into a comprehensive Double Taxation Agreement (DTA) with Hong Kong. At the time of writing, Hong Kong has entered into DTAs with fifty jurisdictions and is in negotiations

94. Further details are contained in Departmental Interpretation and Practice Notes No. 31, available at https://www.ird.gov.hk/eng/pdf/dipn31.pdf.

with sixteen jurisdictions.[95] These prevent double taxation and fiscal evasion, and foster cooperation between Hong Kong and other international tax administrations by enforcing their respective tax laws. A DTA only affects residents of Hong Kong or other DTA jurisdictions.

146. Unless exempted from tax liabilities (for example, any charitable institution or trust of a public character, which is exempt from tax under section 88 of the IRO (*see* below)), income derived from or arisen in Hong Kong from sports activities is charged with profits tax and salaries tax the same way as other commercial entities or tax residents.

IX. Hong Kong Charities

147. Some sports associations are recognized by the IRD as Tax-Exempt Charities under section 88 of the IRO. Exemption of charities from tax is granted by section 88 of the IRO which provides that a charity is exempt from profits tax subject to certain conditions to be fulfilled in relation to the trade or business carried on by the charity concerned. The IRD's role is to ensure that tax exemption is provided to a charity as a tax-exempt charity as per the relevant IRO provisions.

148. A voluntary or a non-profit organization or non-governmental organization (NGO) is not necessarily a charity, however worthy of its causes. In Hong Kong, a charity must be established for exclusive charitable purposes. There is no Hong Kong statutory law governing charities, instead, charities law in Hong Kong has been developed through precedents. In order to be recognized as a charity in Hong Kong, the entity must be established for purposes which are exclusively charitable. According to cases, charitable purposes are classified into four heads. The leading case on the definition of charity is set out in *Commissioners for Special Purposes of Income Tax v. Pemsel.*[96]

149. In that case, the dictum of Lord Macnaghten set out four principal divisions of charitable purposes:

i. the relief of poverty;
ii. the advancement of education;
iii. the advancement of religion; and
iv. other purposes of a charitable nature beneficial to the community not falling under any of the preceding heads.

150. While the purposes under the first three heads (i.e., poverty, education and religion) may be in relation to activities carried on in any part of the world, those under head (iv) will only be regarded as charitable if they are of benefit to the Hong

95. DTAs concluded with Hong Kong https://www.ird.gov.hk/eng/tax/dta_inc.htm.
96. *Income Tax Special Purposes Commissioners v. Pemsel* [1891] AC 531.

Kong community. The courts have considered various situations where charity status was claimed. It should be noted that the courts held that encouragement of a particular sport such as football or cycling or the provision of a playing field or recreation ground are not charitable purposes. Therefore, institutions or sports clubs with the purpose of promoting sports activities are not considered charities and hence subject to taxation in Hong Kong like other business ventures.[97] A list of charitable institutions and trusts of a public character, which are exempt from tax under section 88 of the IRO, is maintained by the IRD.[98]

151. In 2013, the Law Reform Commission of Hong Kong published a report proposing that all Hong Kong charitable organizations should be subject to the requirement of registration. At present, there is neither a formal and established registration system for charitable organizations in Hong Kong nor any specific Government authority that has overall responsibility in this area. The lists of charities, such as the list of charities exempted from tax under section 88 of the IRO is not a comprehensive and conclusive list of all the charities in Hong Kong. Furthermore, it is not compulsory for charities to include their names on this list. Since the publication of the report in 2013, no action has been taken to implement the recommendations under the report.[99]

§4. Principles of Tort Law

I. Civil Liability

Duty of Care

152. A duty of care arises in most scenarios where there are interactions among different entities or people. If one fails to exercise a proper duty of care, one may be held liable for negligence.

153. What then, is a duty of care?

> The case of Donoghue v. Stevenson[100] is a landmark legal precedent on the duty of care. This is an English case that has shaped the development of negligence doctrine in common law jurisdictions, including Hong Kong.

154. In this case, Mrs. Donoghue's friend purchased a ginger beer which came in a dark bottle for her from a café. After consuming half of the bottle, the remaining contents were poured into a tumbler. To Mrs. Donoghue's shock, the decomposed

97. Tax guide for charitable institutions and trusts of a public character https://www.ird.gov.hk/eng/pdf/tax_guide_for_charities.pdf.
98. List of charitable institutions and trusts of a public character, which are exempt from tax under s. 88 of the IRO https://www.ird.gov.hk/eng/tax/ach_index.htm.
99. The Law Reform Commission of Hong Kong Report on Charities https://www.hkreform.gov.hk/en/publications/rcharities.htm.
100. *Donoghue v. Stevenson* [1932] AC 562.

remains of a snail floated out of the bottle. Since Mrs. Donoghue was not able to commence a claim based on breach of contract warranty (as she was not a party to any contract), she initiated legal proceedings against the manufacturer, Stevenson. Having considered the facts, Lord Atkin, the judge presiding over the hearing, pointed out that one must take reasonable care to avoid acts or omissions which he can reasonably foresee likely injury to his "neighbour," where "neighbour" would include persons who are so closely and directly affected by his act that he ought reasonably to have them in contemplation as being so affected when directing his mind to the acts or omissions which are called in question.[101]

155. In order to be liable in the tort of negligence: (1) a duty of care must be owed by the Defendant to the claimant; (2) the Defendant must have breached that duty; (3) the Defendant must have caused the damage,; (4) the damages must not be too remote.

156. Notwithstanding, the criterion of foreseeability and fairness for establishing the duty of care was found inadequate in later cases, leading to the development of the Anns test[102] (which has now been overruled by *Murphy v. Brentwood District Council*[103]) and later the Caparo test, i.e., a duty is imposed only when it would be fair, just and reasonable.[104]

Between Players

157. As stated by Deputy District Judge W K Wong (as he then was) in *Ma Yong Mei v. Cheng Muk Lam,*[105] the standard of care in the sporting context is different from a non-sporting context. This is with reference to the English case of *Blake v. Galloway*, where Dyson LJ stated:

> "that participants in sport games generally owe each other a duty of care and that the standard of care depends on all the circumstances of the case, and that the threshold for liability is high (see para 11)."
>
> "there will be no liability for errors of judgement, oversights or lapses of which any participant might be guilty in the context of a fast-moving contest. Something more serious is required." [106]

158. Deputy District Judge W K Wong (as he then was) also referred to the remarks of Diplock LJ (as he then was) in *Wooldridge v. Sumer & another*[107]

101. *Ibid.*, para. 580.
102. *Anns v. Merton London Borough Council* [1978] AC 728.
103. *Murphy v. Brentwood District Council* [1991] 1 AC 398, [1990] 2 All ER 908 (HL).
104. *Caparo Industries Plc v. Dickman* [1990] UKHL 2.
105. *Ma Yong Mei v. Cheng Muk Lam* [2015] HKCU 2989.
106. *Blake v. Galloway* (2004) 1 WLR 2844 para. 8-11.
107. *Wooldridge v. Sumner & another* [1963] 2 QB 43.

(remarks of which were also applied in the sports injury-related case of *Chan Kin Bun v. Wong Sze Ming & another*[108]):

> a person attending a game or competition takes the risk of any damage caused to him by any act of a participant done in the course of and for the purposes of the game or competition notwithstanding that such acts may involve an error of judgement or lapse of skill, unless the participant's conduct is such as to evince a reckless disregard of the spectator's safety.

159. While the degree of care should be objectively reasonable, a mere error in judgment or a temporary lapse in skill or care is insufficient to establish liability. Consent is the most common defense in sports-related negligence cases and such consent can be either expressed or implied, depending on the circumstances. For instance, in boxing matches (which necessarily include sparring and a lot of physical contact), contestants may have signed waivers prior to the match, releasing the other boxer from any liability of physical injury.

160. Even in the absence of a formal or expressly written agreement entered into prior to a sports competition, the nature and inherent risks associated with the sport may support the Defendant's argument that by participating in the event, the victim has impliedly or by conduct consented to taking inherent risks. It is becoming increasingly common for organizers of competitions to request that participants sign a waiver at the time they register for the competitions, to release the organizers from various liabilities.[109]

161. Therefore, even though players in competitions also owe each other duty of care, under normal circumstances, participants who willingly engaged in a vigorous sport may have impliedly consented to assuming a certain risk of injury. Hence, a higher threshold must be met to establish negligence.[110] For example, where a player is injured during a sporting event, such as being struck by the ball in a soccer game and then suffers a concussion, the court will consider the facts to ascertain if the co-player who kicked the ball had behaved recklessly or intentionally causing harm beyond the scope of normality.[111] If the co-player's action was reckless or intentional, they may be held liable for the breach of duty of care.[112]

---

108. (2006) HKCU 429. In this case, Plaintiff claimed that he was injured during a mock sword flight using T-square rulers. The claim was dismissed.
109. It should be noted that the exclusion of liabilities is subject to certain restrictions and is not an absolute defence to claims.
110. *Dickson Poon v. Kan Wai Yu and The Hong Kong Jockey Club* [2002] HKCU 373; *Ma Yong Mei v. Cheng Muk Lam* [2015] HKEC 2580.
111. *Wooldridge v. Sumner and Another* [1963] 2 QB 43.
112. *Blake v. Galloway* (2004) 1 WLR 2844.

Between Occupier and Players

162. The safety of athletes has always been at the forefront of sports, even in high-risk domains such as motorsports and rugby, as injuries to athletes can severely affect both their long-term performance and mental wellbeing. Injuries can arise for a multitude of reasons, including injury between players, injury from the venue, or possibly from various sources combined. Apart from players themselves, all parties involved in a sporting event, including players, organizers and spectators, will owe a duty of care to each other.

163. There have been cases where severe weather conditions, including torrential rain, thunderstorms, and lightning can affect the competition grounds.

164. In the example of a football game played outdoors on artificial turf, if artificial turf is flooded, it could significantly impact the ability of players to dribble or pass. The deteriorated playing conditions may contribute to an unsafe playing field, resulting in injury to the players. The clarity in the competition rules, the comprehensiveness of the terms governing the use of the premises, and the awareness and sensitivity of the risks by the referees in deciding whether to discontinue a game due to hazardous conditions will be imperative to ensure the safety of the players and the integrity of the match.

165. Broadly, occupiers' liability refers to the duty of care of the owner or leaser (i.e., the occupier) of the premises to ensure their visitors are reasonably safe when using their premises. This is governed by the Occupiers Liability Ordinance (Cap. 314) in Hong Kong, where an occupier who fails to maintain the premises under their control in a safe condition may be liable for any injuries suffered by a visitor. While the U.K. case *Portsmouth Youth Activities Committee v. Poppleton*[113] established that the occupier would rarely be held liable for contributory negligence if the risk of injury in sports is obvious and inherent, in this instance, whether the risk of playing in such weather conditions and on the flooded artificial turf obvious is debatable. Therefore, the occupiers of the football field may be liable for a player who is injured on the artificial turf, which was made unsafe to use in the torrent weather.

166. While injury compensation claims could be covered by occupier's/public liability insurance, such risk of injury could nonetheless have been prevented if the occupiers stipulated under the terms of use of the artificial turf that they reserve the right to suspend the usage of the pitch if the condition deteriorates to an extent deemed unsafe, *inter alia*, due to flooding. Not only could this safeguard the occupier from any liability, but most importantly, it also ensures the safety of those using the occupier's venue.

---

113. *Portsmouth Youth Activities Committee v. Poppleton* [2008] E.W.C.A. Civ 646.

167. Organizers are also expected to take reasonable precautions to ensure that the venue is suitable for the activity and that the tools and equipment used are reasonably safe. The organizers, like the occupiers, have an obligation to exercise duty of care toward both athletes and spectators under the Occupiers' Liability Ordinance (Cap. 314) and common law.[114] This duty of care is one within reason. Furthermore, unless there is reckless conduct on the organizer's part, spectators attending a competition have assumed the risk of any harm caused to them by acts performed by players with adequate skill and competence during the game, even if those acts involve errors in judgment or lapses in skill.[115]

Between coaches/trainers and players

168. In addition to the duty of care in competition, civil liability may arise when a person or entity fails to adequately supervise a sports training.[116] Having regard to the factual matrix, coaches and staff may also be held liable as they are responsible for training athletes in a way that prevents them from harm, and therefore should not recklessly put the athlete at risk. Lastly, it is the responsibility of the event organizer to ensure the facilities satisfy all safety regulations and provide medical care to injured players as shown in *Watson v. British Boxing Board of Control*, where the organizer failed to provide immediate and adequate medical care to treat the player.[117]

169. Some organizations expressly set out the duty of care to ensure athletes in training are not injured. The HKSI, which is the Hong Kong Government's designated organization to provide a high-performance training system for eligible sports, has implemented Hong Kong Sports Institute Staff Code of Ethical Conduct (HKSI SCEC). Pursuant to section B 1.9 of HKSI SCEC, the HKSI has a duty of care to safeguard all children training under its elite training system. Should any children injure themselves during the training, the HKSI may be liable under the tort of negligence.

Defamation

170. Sports have long been a popular hobby for most, with athletes celebrated as idols. With freedom of expression and speech, celebrities have been subject to public opinions and criticism, with news reports surrounding their everyday behavior. Athletes may have their name tarnished by false statements made by inaccurate news reports or online articles and may suffer damages, not only in terms of deteriorated mental health and medical bills but also by way of loss of contract deals due to public backlash.

114. *Watson v. British Boxing Board of Control* [2001] QB 1134.

115. *Chan Kin Bun v. Wong Sze Ming & another* [2006] 3 HKCU 429 [10], *Woolridge v. Sumner* [1963] 2 QB 43.

116. *Leung Sze Nok, A Minor By Her Next Friend Leung Yuen Fat v. Tsuen Wan Properties Limited Trading As Riviera Ice Chalet* [2010] HKCU 1584 [43].

117. Watson v. British Boxing Board of Control [2001] QB 1134.

171. Persons who have suffered as a result of untrue words and gossip may have remedies under the Defamation Ordinance of Hong Kong (Cap 21). Pursuant to section 5 of the Defamation Ordinance, where any person who maliciously publishes any defamatory libel acknowledging it to be false will be held liable, and the Plaintiff may seek damages. Defamation can occur through two methods: libel being permanent such as through forms of audio recording or written statements, and slander being temporary such as an oral statement or gesture. The publication must also be made toward a third party other than the Plaintiff for it to be defamatory.

172. However, one cannot use the threat of defamation to bar all publications or discussions which may appear unfavorable to them. For example, a defamation claim may not succeed under certain circumstances as a matter of public interest. Where freedom of speech clashes with the need to protect one's reputation, the person publishing the information (be it the journalist or editor) may raise the defense of qualified privilege. This defense stems from the need to protect free speech whereby the publisher *objectively* is under the moral duty to disclose and publish the information for public interest. Proving that there was an honest belief that the publisher has a legitimate duty or interest to publish the defamatory content will not on its own suffice to establish the defense.

173. The ultimate question is whether it is in the public interest to publish the statement notwithstanding its defamatory nature. In the case of *Pui Kwan Kay v. Ming Pao Holdings Ltd and Others,*[118] the court held that despite the tone of the article in question could be regarded as "aggressive or even provocative," it was within the editorial judgment in the context of responsible journalism. The court found that the Defendants had established the defense of public interest. Sports commentators or journalists should be careful not to publish unverified material in order to prevent the risk of making a defamatory remark.

Limitation period

174. One should consider that a claim for breach of contract or tort (e.g., defamation) must be brought to Court before the expiry of the six-year limitation from the date when the cause of action accrued, pursuant to section 4 of the Limitation Ordinance (Cap. 347).[119]

Mediation

175. An alternative to commencing a court action is mediation. Mediation is an out-of-court negotiation process for parties to reach a settlement with the facilitation of an independent mediator.

176. A range of organizations in Hong Kong provide professional and comprehensive mediation services whether they are domestic cases, cross-border or international cases. These organizations include but are not limited to Asian-African Legal Consultative Organization-Hong Kong Regional Arbitration Centre

118. *Pui Kwan Kay v. Ming Pao Holdings Ltd & Others* (2015) HKCV 2771
119. Limitation Ordinance (Cap. 347).

(AALCO-HKRAC), the Hong Kong International Arbitration Centre (HKIAC), Centre for Effective Dispute Resolution, Hong Kong International Mediation Centre (HKIMC), Hong Kong Mediation Centre, Hong Kong Mediation and Arbitration Centre, Mainland-Hong Kong Joint Mediation Center, and eBRAM, which is an online mediation service that utilizes artificial intelligence (AI).

177. If an agreement is reached during a mediation, a mediation settlement agreement would be prepared for the parties to sign and record the agreed settlement terms and conditions. Previously, where a breach of that mediation settlement agreement was to occur and such breach is disputed, the parties would have to commence an action in court for breach of contract, to enable the court to adjudicate the issues. Where the parties and issues at play were of an international nature, there were further jurisdictional aspects to consider. As these were problems deterring parties from mediation, the Mediation Convention entered into force on September 12, 2020. Its aim is to allow international settlement agreements resulting from mediation to be recognized and enforced.

178. The Mediation Convention is a treaty signed by multiple countries and forms a "uniform and efficient framework for the enforcement and invocation of international settlement agreements resulting from mediation."[120] The convention serves to be an aid to mediation settlement agreements that are (i) international,[121] and (ii) in commercial settings,[122] usually being cross-border trade disputes. Forty-six countries have signed the convention on the first day, including the PRC and the United States of America, as well as an additional twenty-four countries attended the signing ceremony to give their support. As of June 11, 2024, there are fifty-seven signatories and fourteen parties.

Arbitration

179. Sport arbitration is rapidly developing in Hong Kong. With a robust legal infrastructure and a highly competent legal profession, arbitration in Hong Kong is seamlessly conducted from start to finish, ensuring a high-quality and efficient service throughout the process.

180. The introduction of the Arbitration Ordinance (Cap. 609) in Hong Kong in 2011 marked a significant development in the region's arbitration framework. This ordinance draws heavily from the widely recognized UNCITRAL Model Law on International Commercial Arbitration, which enjoys familiarity among legal practitioners from both civil law and common law jurisdictions, as well as the international business community.

181. The legal landscape in Hong Kong is characterized by a substantial number of reputable legal professionals. As of the end of November 2023, there are over

---

120. *Background of the Convention*, Singapore Convention of Mediation https://www.singaporeconvention.org/convention/about.
121. Article 1(1) Mediation Convention.
122. Article 1(2) Mediation Convention.

1,600 practicing barristers, over 11,000 practicing solicitors and almost 1,500 registered foreign lawyers in Hong Kong.[123] Among them, there are over 200 arbitrators and mediators who are experts in sports.[124] This diverse presence of local and international legal practitioners contributes to Hong Kong's ability to deliver exceptional legal services, ensuring the provision of top-quality assistance to clients.

182. As over 170 countries and regions in the world, the New York Convention applies in Hong Kong (though Hong Kong is not a signatory of the New York Convention, originally applied by the government of the U.K., and after the return of Hong Kong to China, such application was affirmed by the PRC government).[125] This ensures that its arbitral awards are enforceable in all contracting parties.

183. Hong Kong also holds a unique position as the sole common law jurisdiction within China. The implementation of the Interim Measures Arrangement in 2019 has brought about a game-changing impact. Hong Kong became the sole jurisdiction outside Mainland China where parties engaged in arbitral proceedings administered by designated arbitral institutions can seek interim measures from mainland courts to preserve assets, evidence and conduct even before the arbitration award.

184. There are seven qualified institutions for the Interim Measures Arrangement, including AALCO-HKRAC, China International Economic and Trade Arbitration Commission Hong Kong Arbitration Center, eBRAM, HKIAC, Hong Kong Maritime Arbitration Group, International Court of Arbitration of the International Chamber of Commerce - Asia Office and South China International Arbitration Center (HK).[126]

185. There are only currently a handful of organizations which brand themselves as offering Alternative Dispute Resolution (ADR) services for sports-related disputes.

186. The Court of Arbitration for Sport (CAS) was originally established as part of the IOC. CAS offers mediation and arbitration services to settle disputes directly or indirectly related to sport. Under the New York Convention, the arbitral award issued by the CAS is final, binding and enforceable. CAS also provides mediation services with its own set of rules to resolve contractual disputes. CAS has divisions including but not limited to an "Ordinary Arbitration Division," for sole-instance disputes submitted to the CAS, and an "Appeals Arbitration Division," for disputes

123. Eric Chu, *Legal Services Industry in Hong Kong*, HKTDC (Sep. 6, 2024), https://research.hktdc.com/en/article/MzEzODc5NTk5.
124. Department of Justice, *Development of Sports Dispute Resolution in Hong Kong*, DoJ (Sep. 6, 2024), https://www.doj.gov.hk/en/legco/pdf/ajls20240527e1.pdf.
125. There are currently over 172 parties to the New York Convention. Each of these parties undertakes to recognise and enforce the arbitral award made by member states in their domestic courts.
126. The Government of Hong Kong Special Administration Region, *Institutions qualified for interim measure applications announced,* GovHK (Sep. 6, 2024), https://www.info.gov.hk/gia/general/202303/31/P2023033100302.htm.

resulting from final-instance decisions taken by sports organizations. The arbitral procedures are conducted in French or English, though under certain conditions, another language may be used. Similar to other commercial arbitration, the award can only be challenged in the Swiss Federal Court under very limited grounds, including lack of jurisdiction, violation of procedural rules or incompatibility with public policy.[127]

187. China Commission of Arbitration for Sport (CCAS) is another institution offering sports arbitration and mediation. CCAS places its emphasis on ensuring that sports arbitration is conducted independently and in compliance with the law, without interference from any administrative body, social organization, or individual. CCAS specifically focuses on three categories of disputes: (1) disputes arising from dissatisfaction with decisions such as disqualifications, cancellation of competition results, and match suspensions; (2) disputes arising from registration or interactions among athletes; and (3) other disputes that arise within the context of competitive sports activities.

188. AALCO is a significant force contributing to public and private international law developments. It is an inter-governmental organization that was founded in 1956 and now with forty-nine member states comprising the major states from Asia and Africa. Two-thirds of the world's population lives in AALCO member states and the combined gross domestic product (GDP) exceeds many trillions of U.S. dollars.

189. One of the major contributions to the economic field was the introduction of the Integrated Scheme for Settlement of Disputes in Economic and Commercial Transactions in 1978. Pursuant to that Scheme, regional arbitration centers were established under the auspices of AALCO. These centers function as international institutions with the primary goals of promoting international commercial arbitration in the Asian-African regions and facilitating the conduct of international arbitrations. With the establishment of the AALCO-HKRAC in 2021, AALCO now has six international regional arbitration centers.

190. Among others, AALCO has shown significant commitment to sports dispute resolution. Two of the six AALCO Arbitration Centres, namely the Asian International Arbitration Centre (AIAC) in Malaysia and the Cairo Regional Centre for International Commercial Arbitration in Egypt, serve as alternative hearing centers for the CAS.

191. AALCO-HKRAC is another prominent entity in the field of sports dispute resolution. It was established by international law and has operated in Hong Kong since 2022 with backing from the Central Government, and now operates under the

127. "General Information: What is the Court of Arbitration for Sports" Court of Arbitration for Sport, https://www.tas-cas.org/en/general-information/frequently-asked-questions.html.

auspices of forty-nine member state countries. It not only administers sport arbitration and mediation but also offers training programs in sport arbitration to individuals worldwide. It also continues and grows its existing dispute resolution with the SF&OC to build a regional comprehensive legal and dispute resolution system that is unbiased and balances the interest of all parties, be it the players, mega event organizers, or spectators.

192. AALCO-HKRAC strives to build capacity for sports-related dispute resolution lawyers/experts, which could be a new career for professional athletes, and to collaborate with and support the SF&OC to resolve disputes, improve transparency and governance, and to create an overarching legal and dispute resolution framework for the region, that fairly and impartially represents the interest of all parties., including sports associations, athletes, mega event's organizers, spectators, and all without burdening the court system.

193. The establishment of a robust and impartial dispute resolution framework for the sports industry is crucial to ensure the smooth and sustainable development of Hong Kong's sports sector. Multiple countries have already established or are in the process of establishing their own organizations for sports dispute resolution, such as Switzerland's CAS, Malaysia's AIAC, and Japan's Sports Arbitration Agency. Hong Kong could heed this growing development and seize the opportunity to grow and establish Hong Kong's role in resolving sports-related disputes locally and regionally.

194. By leveraging the expertise and neutrality of arbitration centers, Hong Kong can become a geographically convenient and impartial environment that instills confidence and trust among all sports stakeholders. This kind of initiative would align with Hong Kong's reputation as a leading international hub for dispute resolution, further reinforcing the city's attractiveness as a destination for major sports events and competitions.

195. The development of sports arbitration is important for the future growth of the sports industry in Hong Kong and to further strengthen Hong Kong's role in the global sports industry, construct a healthy nation, and build Hong Kong as a leading destination for resolving sports-related disputes, all at the same time reinforcing Hong Kong's reputation as a leading regional arbitration center within the Asia-Pacific region.

Insurance

196. There are many sports insurance products available on the market to protect athletes from injuries. Most of the products in Hong Kong cover sports injuries, personal liabilities and medicinal expenses that occur during the participation of the said sport. Team insurance will normally be purchased by the team, covering around ten to twenty-five players per team.

197. A common complaint with sports insurance is that the insurance payout is capped too low, which is not sufficient to relieve the weight off of athletes' shoulders upon receiving hefty medical bills. There have been ongoing local incidents that solidify this concern in recent years. Therefore, the government and national sports associations should collaborate and outline new guidelines regarding the sum granted by insurance companies to sportspersons in order to ensure that coverage meets the needs arising from sports injuries.

198. Organizers of mega sports events now have to be aware of the growing challenges that may arise from cyber-attacks and physical terrorism. With the looming possibility of militant attacks in uncertain geopolitical climates, organizers will need to plan ahead and ensure they are prepared for event cancellations. Following the rapid development of technology which can create AI-generated fake images, AI may be used to compromise the competition's integrity. These issues, in turn, may result in significant contractual claims and negatively impact the security of the event. Not only should there be appropriate security measures in place to prevent these risks but organizers should also consider obtaining the appropriate insurance to safeguard against such contractual claims.

II. Public Health and Safety

Recreation and Sports Facilities

199. The LCSD provides a range of recreation and sports facilities, aiming to promote the development and engagement with sports within the city.[128] However, given the public nature of LCSD's spaces, the use of leisure facilities is governed by the CULF, which ensures the health and safety of the public and protects the conditions of such spaces. Notably, an important aspect of the CULF is that all hirers/users must comply with the PGR (Cap. 132BC) and adhere to all instructions given by the staff of the LCSD.

200. In order to encourage compliance with the CULF, if any person fails to comply with the conditions of use or instructions given by the LCSD to the LCSD's full satisfaction, the venue management is entitled to cancel the confirmed booking and terminate the use of the facility immediately without compensation. In these circumstances, the applicant/user/hirer must vacate the facility immediately. In relation to the use of pleasure grounds, the LCSD may also remove any person from the facility/venue if he/she is in breach of the PGR or other regulations in force. In such an event, the booking will be canceled automatically and the paid fees forfeited.[129] Ultimately, these rules are in place to ensure that the LCSD's public facilities provide a safe environment for users and that they are used as intended.

128. Mission, Vision and Values, LCSD, https://www.lcsd.gov.hk/en/aboutlcsd/mission.html.
129. *Conditions of Use for Leisure Facilities,* LCSD, https://www.lcsd.gov.hk/en/condition/index.html.

Fitness Rooms

201. To promote well-being in the community, a wide range of leisure facilities are provided by the LCSD, including fitness rooms. However, given the presence of dangerous equipment, such as heavy weights and treadmills, the CULF states that only users with the required qualifications and aged 15 or above, in addition to being registered as a user of fitness rooms under the LCSD, may use the fitness rooms in sports venues.

202. If an individual wishes to access LCSD's fitness rooms, the following conditions are the qualifications required:

a. participate in the "Briefing on Proper Ways to Use Fitness Equipment" and pass the assessment organized by LCSD;
b. participate in the "Fitness (Multi-gym) Training Course" organized by LCSD from May 2006 onward and attain an attendance rate of at least 80%;
c. hold an LCSD Fitness Gold Card; and
d. hold equivalent qualifications recognized by the Physical Fitness Association of Hong Kong, China.[130]

203. These requirements ensure only individuals with the required competence can access potentially dangerous fitness equipment, mitigating physical injuries arising from user ineptitude.

Sports Grounds for Athletic Meets and Other Sports Activities

204. Sports grounds, such as the renowned Hong Kong Stadium (which is the current largest outdoor multi-purpose recreation and sports venue in Hong Kong) and the Kai Tak Sports Park (which is set to become Hong Kong's largest and most comprehensive sports and leisure complex, expected to open in 2025),[131] are some of the most important facilities run by the LCSD. These facilities provide spaces for uses ranging from community leisure and mega concerts to elite international competitions, such as the Hong Kong Sevens, which is a World Rugby stop that attracts a flock of international participants and spectators. Therefore, the usage of sports grounds is regulated under the CULF in order to safeguard the health and safety of the users and the wider community. The rules governing the use of sports grounds are set out under the PGR, and users must also adhere to all instructions given by the management staff of the facilities.

205. In certain circumstances, the LCSD may close a sports ground, as, *inter alia*, it may be deemed unsafe for use, e.g., where usage of an open sports ground may increase the risk of injury through slippage or otherwise. The conditions include:

---

130. *Procedure for Registration—Fitness Rooms,* LCSD, https://www.lcsd.gov.hk/en/fitness/procedure.html.

131. Kai Tak Sports Park's State-of-the-Art Youth Sports Ground Nears Completion Unleashing Hong Kong's Sporting Potential with World-Class Facilities and Natural Turf System—Kai Tak Sports Park.

a. the issuance of tropical cyclone signal no. 8 or above, or the Rainstorm Black Warning;
b. the sports ground is considered unsuitable for usage, for example, through a significantly deteriorated pitch condition;
c. it is operationally expedient to do so; or
d. inclement weather is imminent.

206. For uses involving public admission, temporary structures (excluding those provided by the venue), or those of a high-risk nature, the chance of injury increases significantly. Therefore, the hirer may be required by the District Leisure Manager/ venue manager to obtain suitable insurance coverage for the purpose of protecting the interests of both the hirer and the government. The prevailing level of indemnity set by the LCSD shall be applied to meet the scale/nature of the use/event.

207. By reason of the nature of the use/activity of the hirer, a maximum user capacity of the booked facility may also be stipulated by the management on grounds of public safety and management consideration.

PGR

208. The PGR primarily serves to ensure the venues are used as intended. Under the regulation, there are two sections most relevant to public health and safety—sections 18 and 19.

209. Specifically, PGR section 18 ensures that when any part of the pleasure ground is reserved by the Director of Leisure and Cultural Services for a specified game, only authorized players can play on the specified, reserved area, given they use the pleasure ground to play the game for which it was set aside. In doing so, the provision deters instances of unauthorized entry during the progression of the approved game, ensuring the safety of both the approved players and unauthorized persons. For example, instances of streaking, or pitch invasions during elite international competitions, are strictly prohibited, given it could endanger players and harm Hong Kong's international reputation.

210. Similarly, section 19 of the PGR also serves to protect users of the pleasure ground, ensuring the ground's condition is appropriate for safe usage. By prohibiting the use of pleasure grounds which are deemed unfit for use due to the ground's condition or otherwise, this provision mitigates injuries occurring to players due to playing on unfit grounds, along with further deterioration of the condition of the pleasure ground. Further, by ensuring sports grounds are only used when in good condition, this provision of the PGR can also ensure that Hong Kong sports grounds comply with international standards, further facilitating Hong Kong's vision of becoming a preferred center for hosting major sporting events.

§5. Relationship Between Natural Justice and Sports Justice

211. In Hong Kong, the relationship between natural justice and sports justice is interconnected and complementary. Natural justice refers to the legal system and judicial processes that govern society as a whole, ensuring the rule of law, protection of rights, and resolution of disputes in a fair and impartial manner. However, sports justice pertains to the specific rules, regulations, and disciplinary mechanisms that govern the sports community, ensuring integrity, fairness, and ethical conduct in sports activities.

212. Learning the tactics of the rivals before a sports game may be a common practice that is at the same time debatable. There has been debate on whether this is acceptable behavior. Even though the rules of the games may not specify that such actions are prohibited, the standard of sportsperson and sportsmanship may differ across different cultures and different sports, and deviations in standards may cause dispute and outrage, lead to reputation damage and potentially affect commercial endorsements and sponsorship.

213. While natural justice and sports justice operate within distinct spheres, they share common principles of fairness, accountability, and transparency. The legal framework of Hong Kong provides the foundation for upholding the rule of law and protecting the rights of individuals, including athletes, coaches, officials, and sports organizations. In cases where sports-related disputes or disciplinary matters intersect with legal issues, the principles of natural justice may come into play to ensure that due process is followed, rights are respected, and decisions are made in accordance with the law.

214. Sports justice, however, is tailored to the unique needs and challenges of the sports industry, addressing issues such as doping violations, match-fixing, misconduct, and rule infractions specific to sports competitions. Sports organizations and governing bodies in Hong Kong are responsible for enforcing sports justice through disciplinary procedures, investigations, and sanctions to uphold the integrity and credibility of sports activities.

215. Overall, the relationship between natural justice and sports justice in Hong Kong is characterized by a shared commitment to upholding the principles of fairness, accountability, and integrity in both the legal system and the sports community. By working in tandem, natural justice and sports justice contribute to the promotion of a just, ethical, and inclusive society where the rule of law and the spirit of sportsmanship are upheld. To ensure the integrity of the games and the teams, players are expected to play with integrity, and hosting parties are expected to enforce rules and conduct inquiries and disciplinary actions.

216. Sports are inherently team-based activities, even in individual-centric sports, where an athlete's performance is underpinned by crucial members such as coaching staff, teammates and physiotherapists. Therefore, unprofessional or undisciplined behaviors can have detrimental implications on a team's performance, and the athlete may risk damaging his reputation or career. For example, athletes may be subject to disciplinary action and suspension if they are found to have committed multiple disciplinary breaches, such as unexcused absences from training and a poor attitude toward a coach. It is imperative to note that while individual aptitude is fundamental to a team's success, breaches of discipline can have significant, adverse impacts on team morale, and will incur significant consequences on both the team's performance and the individual athlete's reputation. Athletes should also be aware of any provisions governing their conduct in their contracts or the team's policy, as violations may lead to dismissal from their teams or disqualification from competitions. On the same token, organizations should ensure that their rules are clearly set out so that athletes are aware of these, to ensure due procedure and confidence in the system.

217. The concept of natural justice is discussed on many occasions. Justice can be defined as an abstract system of beliefs and standards prescribing appropriate relationships between people and their fates. Justice moderates the relationship between individuals and the societies to which they belong by encouraging people to regulate their own behavior rather than be constrained by others. It is operationalized through law and legal procedures, as well as less formally in shared norms (e.g., reciprocity) and values (e.g., equality).

218. Although justice is intuitively felt to be objective, is in fact a malleable and fluid construct. In both its formal, codified manifestation and informal mores, justice is a human product. Each culture constructs its own norms by altering what was handed down to it. Individuals and social groups vary not only in the way in which they define justice but also in the degree to which they prioritize it over alternative values such as expedience, practicality, or financial growth.[132]

219. Conception of justice is framed in the form of two principles: each person participating in a practice, or affected by it, has an equal right to the most extensive liberty compatible with a like liberty for all; and second, inequalities are arbitrary unless it is reasonable to expect that they will work out for everyone's advantage, and provided the positions and offices to which they attach, or from which they may be gained, are open to all.[133]

220. Aristotelian definition of justice is previously expressed in a Kluwer-published article on Justice and Game Advantage in Sporting Games. Equals ought to be treated equally, unequals can be treated unequally, and unequal treatment ought to be in reasonable accordance with the inequality in question.[134]

---

132. Susan Clayton & Susan Opotow, *Justice and Identity: Changing Perspectives on What Is Fair*, Personality and Social Psychology Review, 7 n. 4 (2003).
133. John Rawls, *Justice as Fairness,* The Philosophical Review, 67 n. 2 (1958).
134. Sigmund Loland, *Justice and Game Advantage in Sporting Games,* Ethical Theory and Moral Practice, 2 n. 2 (1999).

221. Recognizing that equal treatment to all may result in unfairness under certain circumstances, unequal treatment may be applied but only to the extent that it aligns with the inequality being remedied. For example, in the Olympics, there are two separate segments, one held for athletes with no physical disability, and one held around two weeks later for the athletes with physical impairments.[135] Though some may argue that dividing the athletes based on their health condition for competing in the Olympics and Paralympics could amount to unequally treating the physically challenged by denying their right to compete in the normal Olympics, such division allows athletes to compete in a more fair environment.

222. In any event, the judgment and ethical standard of the officials making the decision, e.g., referees and judges, must be impartial and justified. Where there are arbitral penalties or lack of penalties imposed, the referee's credibility and the fairness and due process of the whole game will be called into question. Sometimes, these questions may escalate into a wider lack of confidence in the organization administering the game. On the same token, where teams wantonly challenge a referee's judgment, their sportsmanship may be called into question.

223. The concept of sports justice has different layers and is commonly linked with social justice.

224. The book *Justice and Game Advantage in Sporting Games*[136] suggests that the common perception of sports as competitive events is tied to their inherent logical structure. What we may call the institutional goal of these practices is to measure, compare, and finally rank the participants according to the performance of athletic skills as defined in the rules of the relevant game. In other words, in sporting games, the predominant distributive norm is meritocratic. The norm of equal treatment, then, becomes a necessary condition for a game to take place. To be able to evaluate the relevant inequalities satisfactorily, participants have to compete on the same terms. All competitors ought to be given equal opportunity to perform.[137]

225. Sports justice can be a dynamic platform for positive change. Sports have long been a platform for unity, competition, and entertainment. However, in recent years, the world of sports has also become a powerful arena for social justice movements. Athletes, teams, and organizations are using their platforms to raise awareness, challenge societal norms, and advocate for equality. The intersection of sports and social justice is a dynamic space that continues to evolve and make significant impacts on society.[138]

---

135. "50 things to know about the paralympic game" (Paris 2024), https://olympics.com/en/paris-2024/information/50-things-to-know-about-the-paralympic-games.
136. *Ibid.*
137. *Ibid.*
138. *Achieving Social Justice in Sports: Breaking Barriers & Inspiring Change*, Yellowbrick (Nov. 8, 2023), https://www.yellowbrick.co/blog/sports/achieving-social-justice-in-sports-breaking-barriers-inspiring-change.

226. Sports justice can be a means to address systemic barriers and injustices. Social justice in sports encompasses a wide range of issues, including racial equality, gender equity, LGBTQ+ rights, disability inclusion, and more. It is about recognizing and addressing the systemic barriers and injustices that exist within the sporting world and using sports as a catalyst for positive change. Historically, sports have mirrored societal inequalities, perpetuating stereotypes and discrimination. However, athletes, teams, and organizations are now actively working to dismantle these barriers and create a more inclusive and equitable sporting landscape.[139] For example, during the inaugural Olympic Games in 1896, women were not allowed to compete, but by 1900, women gained the right to compete in a limited number of events, specifically golf, tennis, sailing, croquet and equestrian. This situation gradually improved with increasing consciousness for gender equality, and by 2012, female athletes could compete in all Olympic sports. Since 1991, the inclusion of women's categories has been mandatory for any new sport seeking to be added to the Olympic program.[140]

227. In Hong Kong, sport justice may refer to the fair and impartial resolution of disputes, disciplinary matters, and ethical issues within the sports community. Sports organizations, governing bodies, and regulatory bodies play a crucial role in upholding the principles of sport justice by enforcing rules, regulations, and codes of conduct to ensure integrity, transparency, and accountability in sports activities. These entities are responsible for investigating allegations of misconduct, rule violations, and unethical behavior, and for meting out appropriate sanctions or penalties when necessary.

228. Sport justice in Hong Kong is guided by principles of due process, procedural fairness, and respect for the rights of all parties involved. Athletes, coaches, officials, and other stakeholders in the sports community are expected to adhere to high standards of conduct, sportsmanship, and ethical behavior, and to cooperate with the authorities in upholding the integrity of sports competitions and events. By promoting and upholding sport justice, Hong Kong aims to maintain a level playing field, protect the rights and interests of participants, and preserve the reputation and credibility of the sports industry. Through a commitment to fairness, accountability, and transparency, sport justice in Hong Kong contributes to the promotion of a healthy, ethical, and inclusive sports culture that benefits athletes, fans, and the broader community.

229. In respect of the relationship between natural justice and sports justice in Hong Kong, to uphold the spirit of sports and the values it embodies which include ethics, fair play and honesty among others, measures that strive to uphold the principles of sports justice and create a level playing field in Hong Kong include anti-doping programs and sporting league rules against potential misconduct such as

---

139. *Ibid.*

140. "History and Origin of the games: When did women first compete in the Olympic Games?" (International Olympics Committee) https://olympics.com/ioc/faq/history-and-origin-of-the-games/when-did-women-first-compete-in-the-olympic-games?os=0SLw57pSD&ref=app.

betting and bribery. The need to enhance transparency in the selection of athletes to represent Hong Kong is also highlighted. Generally speaking, commission of the aforementioned offenses and rule violations warrants the initiation of strict disciplinary procedures including but not limited to a fine, suspension, ineligibility for future selection, or appearances before relevant disciplinary committees to answer to the breach.

230. Different federations and associations in Hong Kong have made progress in promoting sports justice in Hong Kong.

231. The Anti-Doping Rules of the SF&OC contain rules on anti-doping. The spirit of sport is expressed in how we play true. Doping is fundamentally contrary to the spirit of sport. Anti-doping programs are founded on the intrinsic value of sport. This intrinsic value is often referred to as "the spirit of sport": the ethical pursuit of human excellence through the dedicated perfection of each athlete's natural talents. Anti-doping programs seek to protect the health of athletes and to provide the opportunity for athletes to pursue human excellence without the use of prohibited substances and prohibited methods. Anti-doping programs seek to maintain the integrity of sport in terms of respect for rules, other competitors, fair competition, a level playing field, and the value of clean sport to the world. The Anti-Doping Rules express that the spirit of sport is the celebration of the human spirit, body and mind. It is the essence of Olympism and is reflected in the values we find in and through sport, including: [141]

a. health;
b. ethics, fair play and honesty;
c. athletes' rights as set forth in the Code;
d. excellence in performance;
e. character and education;
f. fun and joy;
g. teamwork;
h. dedication and commitment;
i. respect for rules and laws;
j. respect for self and other participants;
k. courage; and
l. community and solidarity.

232. There is also a continuing need to enhance transparency in selecting athletes to participate in international games. In December 2011, the BPR was drawn up by the ICAC in consultation with the Home and Youth Affairs Bureau, LCSD and some NSAs. Under the BPR, a set of best practices is provided to enhance the transparency in the selection of athletes to participate in sports games. The audit examined the extent to which the SF&OC had implemented the BPR best practices

141. "WADA Ethics Panel: Guiding Values in Sport and Anti-Doping," World Anti-Doping Agency https://www.wadaama.org/sites/default/files/resources/files/wada_ethicspanel_setofnorms_oct2017_en.pdf (assessed on Aug. 2, 2024).

on transparency in selecting athletes for participating in international games. The audit found that, up to February 29, 2020, some of the best practices were yet to be implemented. Moreover, the Audit found that in a case in 2018, there is scope for enhancing transparency and accountability in selecting athletes to participate in an international game.[142]

233. In 2021, twenty-three swimmers from China tested positive for trimetazidine (TMZ), which is a banned substance for athletes. This happened seven months before the Tokyo Olympics, and there was huge controversy over their eligibility for the Olympics. However, the China Anti-Doping Agency cleared these swimmers of any wrongdoing as they determined the results of TMZ were due to the consumption of food contaminated with TMZ.[143]

234. According to Chinese Anti-Doping Agency (CADA) and World Anti-Doping Agency (WADA), the TMZ found in the contaminated food is due to the ingestion of banned substances used for growth promotion for farm animals such as clenbuterol.[144]

235. The U.S. Anti-Doping Agency accused the WADA of conspiring with the CADA to hide these positive results. The WADA has in return accused the U.S. of defamatory actions, and the U.S. responded by giving the White House the power to cut WADA's funding.[145] Therefore, WADA threatened to launch legal action against the U.S. for defamation. However, the case is still ongoing, and results remain to be seen.

HKFA

236. The HKFA has implemented strict regulations that strive to uproot sporting misconduct primarily including offenses of betting and bribery, and match-fixing behavior and preservation of sporting justice on the local football scene.

237. For instance, the ICAC charged three football players and a betting agent in February 2024 for allegedly bribing football players to rig the results of a number of matches involving three local football clubs participating in the Hong Kong Premier League and the First Division of Hong Kong in two seasons between 2021 and 2023 so as to facilitate syndicate members to profit from illegal gambling.[146]

238. There was also an instance where a football coach accused a female referee of lacking physical fitness after their 1-0 loss to Pegasus in the Premier League and

---

142. SF&OC, *Executive Summary*, https://www.aud.gov.hk/pdf_e/e74ch02sum.pdf.
143. *Tokyo 2020 Olympics: Chinese swimmers were cleared to compete despite failed drug tests*, BBC Sport, Apr. 22, 2021, https://www.bbc.com/sport/swimming/68863337.
144. *Why the world's anti-doping agency feels stuck between US and China*, BBC News, Aug. 1, 2024 https://www.bbc.com/news/articles/cv2gygj1d28o.
145. *Ibid.*
146. ICAC, "ICAC's operation 'Green Grass': Four footballers and betting agent charged for bribery over match-fixing and illegal gambling" Press Release, Feb. 15, 2024, accessed Mar. 1, 2024, available at https://www.icac.org.hk/en/press/index_id_1818.html.

pleaded with the HKFA not to assign female referees to future games. The coach and the defender were handed 10-match bans by the HKFA for offensive and discriminatory behavior, the minimum penalty possible in the circumstances. At HKFA's disciplinary committee meeting, both men were found guilty of misconduct during the Hong Kong Premier League match.[147]

239. Rules of the HKFA contain articles on anti-bribery. For instance, Article 23(4) (Misconduct-Betting and Bribery) of the Rules of the HKFA provides that:

a. No official of an Association or Club, Referee, Assistant Referee, player or Member shall bet on any football match. Member Associations and Member Clubs shall actively enforce this Rule.
b. No Association or Club, or any player, official or member of any Association or Club shall offer or accept or attempt to offer, either directly or indirectly, any consideration whatever to another Club, player or players of any other Club, with a view to influencing the result of a match.

240. Article 24 also contains anti-bribery provisions:

1. No Association, League, Combination, Club, Director, Official or player (in this Rule called the "Member") shall commit or assist in the commission of any of the following acts:
   a. Violation of the Laws of the Game or the Rules, Regulations or By-Laws of this Association or any of them.
   b. Violation of any of the Rules, Regulations or By-Laws of any Association, League or Combination affiliated with the Association or sanctioned by its Board.
   c. Playing with or against any suspended Association, Club or player or being a Director or Official of any suspended association or club.
   d. Being a Bookmaker or Assistant to a Bookmaker or in any other way directly connected with the organizing of Betting Lotteries, Coupon Football Betting or the like without the written consent of the Association.
   e. Displaying in any Club Programme or Publication or on the ground or premises of any Club any advertisement in connection with Betting, Bookmaking, Coupon Football Betting, Football Pools, or other like matters without the written consent of the Association.
   f. Allowing a Director, Official or Player under suspension to act as Referee or in any other capacity relating to the playing or management of football PROVIDED that in the case of a player, he shall be allowed to take part in a training session organized either by the Association or his Club unless decided otherwise by the Board or the Disciplinary Committee.

147. Chan Kin-wa, "Hong Kong football sexism row: Happy Valley coach and player banned for minimum 10 games for discriminatory and offensive behaviour," (South China Morning Post, April 2021) https://www.scmp.com/sport/football/article/3130223/hong-kong-football-sexism-row-happy-valley-coach-and-player-banned (assessed on Sep. 25, 2024).

241. The relationship between natural justice and sports justice in Hong Kong is a delicate balance, evolving with the changes in societal values, and there are challenges and opportunities for promoting and upholding both forms of justice in the sports community. The common principles of fairness, accountability, and transparency that underpin both natural justice apply throughout sports justice, and fairness can only be achieved if all participants follow the relevant rules, regulations, and mechanisms that govern the sports industry. By fostering a culture of justice and ethics in sports, Hong Kong can contribute to the advancement of a just, healthy, and harmonious society where the rule of law and the spirit of sportsmanship are respected and celebrated.

§6. Sports and Criminal Law

Application

242. The law of the place where a crime occurs will be the law of the applicable criminal proceedings. Hong Kong, like other common law jurisdictions, has adopted the "territoriality principle."[148] In general, whenever the whole or part of a criminal act takes place within Hong Kong, the Hong Kong criminal laws will apply. To be convicted of a crime in Hong Kong courts, the prosecution will have to provide proof beyond reasonable doubt that the Defendant had committed the crime.

Contracts excluding criminal liability invalid

243. A contract cannot validly exclude liability for criminal acts, nor the law of the place where the criminal act is to take place.

244. If parties attempt to exclude criminal acts, those provisions will be struck out for illegality if brought to the court. In the event that a clause drafted with the intention of excluding criminal liability is struck out for being illegal and unenforceable, the principle of severability may enable the other terms of a contract to remain valid and enforceable. Therefore, the drafting of a contract is of extreme importance, where it is unclear if some actions for contracts with an international element may be illegal by way of public policy where the service provided is in such a jurisdiction.

245. Adopting the blue-pencil test in the English case, *Sadler v. Imperial Life Assurance Co of Canada,*[149] the *Midland* case[150] has clearly set out three requirements to apply the severability clause, which are: (1) the unenforceable provision is capable of being removed without the necessity of adding to or modifying the wording of what remains; (2) the remaining terms continue to be supported by adequate consideration; and (3) the removal of the unenforceable provision does not so

148. *The jurisdiction of Hong Kong National Security Law,* The Government of the HKSAR, https://www.info.gov.hk/gia/general/202307/06/P2023070600680.htm#:~:text=In%20general%2C%20the%20criminal%20law,international%20law%20and%20international%20practice.

149. *Sadler v. Imperial Life Assurance Co of Canada* [1988] IRLR 388.

150. *Midland* case [2006] HKCU 460.

change the character of the contract that it becomes not the sort of contract that the parties entered into at all. Following the *Midland* case, *Universe Artiste Management Limited v. Kong Yi Ching Elanne and Another*[151] also applied the blue-pencil test, severing an unenforceable clause in the artiste management contract signed by the Defendant (the artiste) and the Plaintiff that states that the artiste must not become pregnant during the period of the contract. As the rest of the contract is enforceable, it was not affected by the severance and remains valid.

246. Therefore, athletes, referees, coaches, and sports institutions must act in compliance with the criminal laws of Hong Kong. This chapter will discuss some criminal offenses that may appear in the field of sports.

I. Corruption and Bribery

247. In an ideal world, sports, especially at the elite level, should be based on a meritocracy, where the phrase "may the best person win" stands true. While this may not always be reflected in the real world, due to externalities such as genuine favoritism, certain illegal behaviors can significantly threaten the ethics of competition, leading to unfair outcomes.

248. As fair competition is a fundamental tenet of sports, without it, the reputation, integrity and legitimacy of the industry will be gravely affected. However, a significant issue inhibiting fair competition is the act of bribery. Given the monetary incentive, those in power may act arbitrarily or seek to actively alter rules, or passively "turn a blind eye" to instances of misconduct for the benefit of the briber, such as banned performance-enhancing substance use, or match-fixing. Therefore, the integrity of a sports game can be impacted if parties do not play by the rules or if they engage in corruption and take bribes to rig the results.

249. The primary source of Hong Kong's anti-corruption laws is the POBO (Cap. 201). The main law enforcement agency in Hong Kong responsible for the enforcement of the POBO is the ICAC.

250. The key provisions concerned are sections 9(1) and (2) of the POBO, which makes it an offense for a person or agent who, without lawful authority or reasonable excuse, solicits or accepts any advantage as an inducement to or reward for or otherwise on account of his (a) doing or forbearing to do, or having done or forborne to do, any act in relation to his principal's affairs or business; or (b) showing or forbearing to show, or having shown or forborne to show, favor or disfavor to any person in relation to his principal's affairs or business.[152]

251. Under section 2 of the POBO, "advantage" is defined as: (a) any gift, loan, fee, reward or commission consisting of money or of any valuable security or of

151. *Universe Artiste Management Limited v. Kong Yi Ching Elanne and Another* [2022] HKCFI 443.
152. Section 9, Cap. 201 POBO.

other property or interest in property of any description; (b) any office, employment or contract; (c) any payment, release, discharge or liquidation of any loan, obligation or other liability, whether in whole or in part; (d) any other service, or favor (other than entertainment), including protection from any penalty or disability incurred or apprehended or from any action or proceedings of a disciplinary, civil or criminal nature, whether or not already instituted; (e) the exercise or forbearance from the exercise of any right or any power or duty; and (f) any offer, undertaking or promise, whether conditional or unconditional, of any advantage within the meaning of any of the preceding paragraphs (a), (b), (c), (d) and (e).

252. One notable case law that applied section 9 of the POBO is *HKSAR v. Chan Siu Man.*[153] In this case, the head of a sports association (first Defendant) allegedly conspired with an athlete (second Defendant) (who allegedly had a positive doping test) to bribe the Secretary-General of the association in order to shorten or lift the athlete's two-year competition ban. The Defendants were convicted and appealed the conviction. The second applicant's conviction was quashed in the appeal, as it was his case, *inter alia*, that he thought money was paid as a fine, instead being a bribe, and the prosecution could not satisfy the court otherwise beyond a reasonable doubt. However, the first applicant's conviction was maintained.

253. As the investigator for all corruption-related matters, the ICAC has been aware of this type of problem and has organized anti-bribery talks for staff of different sports entities, such as the HKFA and stakeholders of football matches, including players and managerial staff of clubs, to raise awareness and understanding on the POBO, handling of conflict of interest and the importance of fair competition.[154]

254. In another case, an ex-manager of the HKJC was charged by the ICAC with bribery for favoring a co-organizer of equestrian events and was jailed for six months. In that case, the Defendant was delegated by the HKJC to negotiate the agreement terms and event details with the co-organizer of an annual world-class equestrian event. During the negotiations, the Defendant was given a watch valued at HKD 8,200 from the son of the co-organizer's director, which he accepted. In return, the Defendant increased the HKJC's sponsorship for two additional programs. The Defendant did not disclose to the HKJC the acceptance of the watch. The ICAC investigation also revealed that the expense claim forms contained certain false statements.[155] The Defendant was found guilty of four charges in violation of the POBO and was sentenced to six months' imprisonment.

255. The above cases all had a detrimental impact on the reputation of the Hong Kong sports industry. However, the following case involving a former Hong Kong

153. [2011] HKCU 1658.

154. ICAC, Hong Kong—Press Releases—ICAC's operation "Green Grass": Four footballers and betting agent charged for bribery over match-fixing and illegal gambling.

155. *Six months' jail for ex-manager of HKJC charged by ICAC with bribery for favouring co-organizer of equestrian events*, ICAC of the HKSAR, https://www.icac.org.hk/en/p/press/index_id_1852.html.

Footballer of the Year pocketing cash to fix two matches was arguably the most shocking to stakeholders of the football circle. On March 23, 2016, Hong Kong's Footballer of the Year in 2009 and club Pegasus' coach at the time of the incident, was approached by club Rangers' then defender prior to a game between the two clubs. He then provided certain instructions in an attempt to fix the match. As a result, the Defendant, along with four other players, was bribed a total of HKD 60,000. On April 13, 2016, the Defendant attempted to fix another match, signaling to one of his players by adjusting the hood of his jacket, but failed to do so as his team won. The Defendant was sentenced to 180 hours of community service. During sentencing, the judge acknowledged that while such offenses are usually not punished by community service, the Defendant's decent background, along with having already been remanded for six months since his guilty plea, and good reports from probation officers, amounts to an exceptional circumstance that justifies this sentence.[156]

256. While most bribery cases involve the match-fixer benefitting monetarily, players can still be imprisoned for match-fixing behavior even if they do not benefit financially. This was evidenced in a Hong Kong case involving a Croatian soccer player, who was a former player of Happy Valley Football Club. He cooperated with his team's sponsor, and deputy manager to fix a First Division League game with Royal Southern. Having adhered to the team's sponsor's half-time instruction, he intentionally played at a level below his best abilities, leading to Happy Valley losing the game. However, there was no evidence showing the player had gained financially.[157]

257. When interviewed under caution by the ICAC, the player admitted that he did not play to his best abilities pursuant to instructions from the deputy team manager, requesting that the match must be lost in the second half and that he also admitted that as a professional football player for multiple years, he knew he should always play to his best abilities. Accordingly, the player was convicted on a count of conspiracy to defraud the HVAA and the HKFA, contrary to the common law. The Magistrate stated that match-fixing is not tolerated and will be dealt with severely by the court. The Croatian player was sentenced to twelve months in jail.

II. Sexual Harassment

258. Sexual harassment has long been a sensitive topic of debate in the global sports communities. As elite competitors strive for glory on the international stage, they should be given the opportunity to focus on their training and performance

156. *Former Hong Kong Footballer of the Year Lee Wai-Lim spared jail in match-fixing* case, South China Morning Post, https://www.scmp.com/news/hong-kong/hong-kong-law-and-crime/article/2144661/former-hong-kong-footballer-year-lee-wai-lim.

157. *Croation soccer player Sasa Mus jailed for match-fixing,* South China Morning Post, https://www.scmp.com/news/hong-kong/article/1662969/croatian-soccer-player-sasa-mus-jailed-match-fixing.

without the added burden of fending off inappropriate advances. It is not only athletes who may fall victim to this type of inappropriate treatment but some coaches and trainers or other persons within the sports industry may also face similar troubles. Persons facing such unacceptable treatment will not only have their rights violated but their mental health and well-being may also take a heavy toll.

259. Various Hong Kong laws protect persons against sexual harassment.

260. The Crimes Ordinance (Cap. 200) has provisions on indecent assault, such as section 122, which states that a person who indecently assaults another person shall be guilty of an offense and shall be liable on conviction on indictment to imprisonment for ten years.

III. Common Assault

261. In Hong Kong, common assault is defined as an act where a person intentionally or recklessly causes another to apprehend immediate and unlawful personal violence, which includes unlawful and non-consensual physical contact. It is both a common law crime,[158] and a statutory offense under section 40 of the Offences Against the Person Ordinance (Cap. 212).[159] The assault need not result in the physical injury of the person assaulted. The elements of the offense are only that a person intentionally or recklessly applies unlawful force to the victim.[160] This does not require actual physical injury; even a missed punch can constitute an offense. A threat of physical harm (accompanied by some actions) or an actual touching of the victim could potentially amount to assault. The maximum penalty for common assault is one year of imprisonment.[161] Defenses such as consent and self-defense are available and cases are typically tried in the Magistrates' Court.

262. In a sports context, common assault could potentially occur if an athlete intentionally or recklessly causes another player to fear immediate unlawful force outside the normal rules and expectations of the sport. However, as players generally consent to a certain level of physical contact within the rules of the game, it is an important factor in sports.

263. If there are actual fights between players or other stakeholders, and those lead to serious injury, the persons involved may be liable under section 17 of the Offences Against the Person Ordinance (Cap. 212) for shooting or attempting to shoot or wounding or striking with intent to do grievous bodily harm.

---

158. Common law offenses are offenses that are not defined by legislation. These would be laws established by case law.
159. Cap. 212 Offenses against the Person Ordinance, https://www.elegislation.gov.hk/hk/cap212!en?pmc=1&m=1&pm=0.
160. *R v. Williams* [1984] 78 Cr App Rep 276; *A-G v. Chan Yuen Lung & Ors* [1989] 1 HKC 470.
161. III. Possible criminal charges against a stalker under the Offences against the Person Ordinance, Family Clic, https://familyclic.hk/en/topics/daily-lives-legal-issues/stalking/possible-criminal-charges-against-a-stalker-under-the-offences-against-the-person-ordinance/.

264. Organizers should ensure that the necessary security personnel are properly stationed during sports competitions, especially where there is a history of sports crowds getting rowdy in those games. Police should be notified if there are any fights or threats of violence on the sports grounds. Proper terms and conditions of entry and use of the sports grounds (including the audience stands) should be prepared to protect the organizers and remind the users of the sports grounds to adhere to orderly and respectful engagement.

IV. Online Abuse and Threats

265. In some instances, individuals such as professional athletes may be subject to comments of a defamatory or extremely critical nature or threats through, *inter alia*, social media and websites, which may cause psychological stress and reputational damage to them. In these cases, the individuals may consider whether the threats should be reported to the police and consider blocking or restricting the access of the commenter or make a request to the platform to alert them of the harmful content published, as the published content may be in breach of the platform's terms of use in addition to injuring the victim.

266. Various sports teams' managers and organizers should also consider ways to protect sports players. They should encourage players to report threats and online abuse. The sports teams' managers and organizers who manage websites or other platforms where comments can be posted should also establish Terms of Service on their websites and clearly convey to all users that they reserve certain rights to remove content, and they should ensure that proper training and support is offered to their players and personnel who may fall victim to such online abuse or threat.

V. Defamation

267. Under certain circumstances, it may be a criminal offense to publish defamatory remarks.

268. Section 5 of the Defamation Ordinance (Cap. 21) sets out the criminal offense:

> **Publishing libel known to be false**
>
> Any person who maliciously publishes any defamatory libel, knowing the same to be false, shall be liable to imprisonment for 2 years, and, in addition, to pay such fine as the court may award.[162]

269. The prosecution will have to establish beyond reasonable doubt that there was the knowledge that the information was false and yet was still published.[163]

162. Section 5, Cap. 21. Defamation Ordinance.
163. For more details on the elements of defamation, please *see* Defamation chapter.

VI. Gambling

270. Gambling is an age-old practice, and gambling on sports results is a very popular pastime for sports fans.

271. Hong Kong has a very controlled gambling environment. Hong Kong prohibits all gambling activities except those authorized by the government.

272. Despite the restrictions, Hong Kong has developed a well-established gambling scene, predominately run by the HKJC.

273. The HKJC provides three types of betting: horse racing, lottery tickets and also football betting. According to their annual report ended June 2024, the club had a betting and lottery revenue of HKD 43.1 billion, with HKD 10.2 billion of approved donations to our Hong Kong communities, benefitted 173 charitable and community projects in 2023/24.[164] As the HKJC Charities Trust is one of the world's top ten charity donors, the club managed to contribute continuously to the local community through different means under their ongoing project such as carrying out the "Jockey Club Community eHealth Care Project"[165] to allow the elderly to better understand their health conditions and "LevelMind@JC"[166] to promote mental health awareness and to cater 12-24-year-old youths by collaborating with non-governmental organizations to encourage youths to seek help when needed.[167]

274. Other than the HKJC, other entities can apply to seek an exemption under the Gambling Ordinance (Cap. 148) to engage in gambling activities.

275. Gambling, which includes gaming, betting and bookmaking, is mostly illegal under the Gambling Ordinance. However, there are exceptions depending on the setting and venue.

276. Gaming is defined as the playing of or at any game for winnings in money or other property whether or not any person playing the game is at risk of losing any money or other property.[168] It could be lawful if the game is played privately on a social occasion and as long the event is not for the purpose of trade or business or for the private gain of any person,[169] or when the game involves dice, dominoes,

164. The HKJC "Annual Report for the year ending 30 June 2024: Acting for the Betterment of Our Society" pp. 6–7, https://corporate.hkjc.com/corporate/english/history-and-reports/2024/index.aspx#8.
165. The HKJC Charities Trust, "Background" (Jockey Club Community eHealth Care Project) https://www.jc-ehealth.hk/en/about/, accessed Jul. 18, 2024.
166. The HKJC Charities Trust, "About Us" (LevelMind2@JC) https://www.levelmind.hk/project-model, accessed Jul. 18, 2024.
167. The HKJC, "Charities" (The HKJC) https://corporate.hkjc.com/corporate/english/who-we-are/charities.aspx, accessed Jul. 18, 2024.
168. Section 2 of the Gambling Ordinance.
169. Section 3(2) of the Gambling Ordinance.

mahjong, playing cards or tin kau tiles that are either played on a social occasion in a restaurant licensed under the Public Health and Municipal Services Ordinance (Cap. 132),[170] in locations where the sale of intoxicating liquor is permitted by a license or other authorization obtained under any ordinance; or in a club-house which has certificate of exemption[171] or compliance.[172] Gaming could also be lawful if the organization hosting the game and conduct is authorized by license under section 22 of the Gambling Ordinance, and is a game of amusement with prizes, tombola or a trade promotion competition.

277. Betting could only be lawful if the bet made does not involve a bookmaker. Bookmaking means soliciting, receiving, negotiating or settling a bet by way of trade or business whether personally or by letter, telephone, telegram or online medium (including the service commonly known as the Internet) or by any other means.[173] This includes raffles, sweepstakes, and anything in competition for money and involves guessing or estimating the result of future events. Moreover, those who provide money or any other property as consideration knowingly for unlawful gambling or an unlawful lottery of another person,[174] promote,[175] sell or own unlawful lottery tickets[176] will also commit an offense under the Gambling Ordinance.

278. Those who engage in bookmaking or have the bet placed by a person in Hong Kong,[177] or facilitate bookmaking will be liable on summary conviction to a fine of HKD 5,000,000 and to imprisonment for two years,[178] or conviction on indictment to a fine of HKD 5,000,000 and to imprisonment for seven years.[179] Betting with a bookmaker or receiving the bet within or outside Hong Kong is an offense and will be subject to imprisonment increasing from three months on the first conviction,[180] to nine months for the third conviction or above,[181] and a fine from level 3 to level 5.

279. In *Hong Kong v. Chu Kam Yiu,*[182] the court held that the offense of bookmaking involves more than receiving a bet, most significantly in the case of betting among friends. There are mainly two elements:

1. that the opportunity for gain or the risk of loss, arose upon him physically receiving the bet from the punter; and

170. Section 3(3)(a)(i) of the Gambling Ordinance.
171. Sections 4(2)(a) Clubs (Safety of Premises) Ordinance.
172. Sections 4(2)(b) Clubs (Safety of Premises) Ordinance.
173. Section 2 of the Gambling Ordinance.
174. Section 14 of the Gambling Ordinance.
175. Section 9 of the Gambling Ordinance.
176. Section 10 of the Gambling Ordinance.
177. Section 7(1) of the Gambling Ordinance.
178. Section 7(c) of the Gambling Ordinance.
179. Section 7(d) of the Gambling Ordinance.
180. Section 8(a) of the Gambling Ordinance.
181. Section 8(c) of the Gambling Ordinance.
182. [2002] HKCU 1424.

2. that his position in respect of the outcome of the event upon which the bet was made, was the opposite to the position of the punter.

Other relevant factors include the set-up and the operation in question, the nature of the activities, the records kept and the equipment used.

280. Therefore, companies who intend to conduct gambling-related business should be mindful of the Gambling Ordinance and ensure that the proper authorizations are obtained prior to commencing such businesses.

Part II. Private Sports Organizations and Their Regulations

281. Regulations and guidelines issued by sports governing bodies, such as the NOC play a significant role in shaping the legal framework for sports in the region.

§1. National Olympic Committee

282. The Amateur Sports Federation & Olympic Committee of Hong Kong was established in 1950. It was formally recognized as a member of the IOC in 1951, then as a member of the Olympic Council of Asia (OCA) in 1952, and finally recognized as a member of EAGA in 1991. The Committee is responsible for the participation of the Hong Kong Delegation to the Olympic Games, Asian Games and East Asian Games.

283. According to the articles of association of the SF&OC,[183] the SF&OC is a non-governmental and non-profit-making organization, of unlimited duration, which is duly registered as a legal entity and exercises its jurisdiction over the territory of Hong Kong, China. It operates in accordance with the Olympic Charter, these articles and the applicable laws in Hong Kong, China.

284. The Amateur Sports Federation & Olympic Committee of Hong Kong was renamed SF&OC on March 8, 1999. Currently, it has a total of eighty-three local member associations, i.e., NSA under SF&OC. NSA is responsible for organizing and managing sports activities in its own field in Hong Kong.

285. As a NOC under the management of elected officers, SF&OC works closely with NSAs to promote and develop sports.

286. The elected officers of SF&OC and NSAs shall uphold the autonomy of the NOC/NSAs, guaranteeing that athletes have a fair and impartial opportunity to participate in competitions. They should also ensure Hong Kong citizens can enjoy high-quality sports and leisure activities.

183. Sports Fed'n & Olympic Comm. of H.K., China, Articles of Association (January 2019), https://www.hkolympic.org/wp-content/uploads/2019/01/Articles-of-Association-of-SFOC-company-limited-by-guarantee.pdf.

287. Through SF&OC, Hong Kong elite athletes are able to receive Olympic Solidarity Scholarships and financial assistance for their local and overseas training. In addition, SF&OC has handed out the Hong Kong Sports Stars Awards each year since 2000 to pay tribute to outstanding athletes.

288. Financial support has also been offered to outstanding coaches who, through nominations, may receive top-level training overseas.

289. Under SF&OC, the Hong Kong Olympic Academy provides free training courses to sports leaders, administrative executives, coaches and technicians.

I. Main Regulations

290. As an NOC, SF&OC is dedicated to the development and promotion of sports in accordance with the Olympic Charter, which serves as the statute for the IOC.

§2. Major National Federations

The SC

291. The SC was established on January 1, 2005, with the task of advising the Hong Kong Government on sports matters such as: (a) the policies, strategies and implementation framework for sports development; and (b) the provision of funding and resources to sports development, with reference to input from stakeholders involved by way of partnership and collaboration.

292. There are three committees under the SC,[184] namely:

a. Community Sports Committee, which provides advice to the SC to relay to the Secretary for Culture, Sports and Tourism (SCST) ways to promote wider participation in sport through a partnership with different sectors of the community, and to consider funding priorities for supporting community sports programs and initiatives;
b. the Elite Sports Committee, which provides advice to the SC to relay to the SCST on high-performance sport issues, provides policy direction to the HKSI, and advises on funding priorities for supporting high-performance sport and athletes; and
c. the Major Sports Events Committee which provides advice to the SC to relay to the SCST on strategies and initiatives for hosting major sports events through partnership with sports associations, the tourism industry and the private sector, and consider funding priorities for major sports events.

184. "Introduction," Sports Commission Hong Kong SAR, https://www.sportscommission.hk/eng/index.htm (assessed Sep. 26, 2024).

293. There are various member associations under the SF&OC.

294. In Hong Kong, there are several major national federations governing various sports disciplines. Some of the prominent national federations are discussed below.

295. HKFA: The HKFA is responsible for overseeing and promoting football in Hong Kong. It organizes domestic leagues, national teams, and grassroots development programs to nurture talent and promote the sport at all levels.

296. HKBA: The HKBA is the governing body for badminton in Hong Kong. It organizes tournaments, training programs, and coaching initiatives to support the growth and development of badminton players in the region.

297. Hong Kong China Tennis Association (HKTA): The HKTA is the national federation for tennis in Hong Kong. It coordinates tennis events, training camps, and player development initiatives to enhance the competitiveness of Hong Kong tennis players on the international stage.

298. HKRU: The HKRU oversees rugby union in Hong Kong, including both the men's and women's national teams. It promotes rugby at all levels, from grassroots to elite, and organizes local leagues, tournaments, and community outreach programs.

299. Hong Kong, China Association of Athletics Affiliates (HKAAA): The HKAAA is the governing body for athletics in Hong Kong. It organizes track and field events, cross-country races, and road races, as well as training programs for athletes of all ages and abilities.

300. These national federations play a crucial role in the development and promotion of their respective sports in Hong Kong, providing opportunities for athletes to compete, excel, and represent the region on the global stage.

301. Tier A Sports Associations include the following:

a. HKAAA
b. HKBA
c. Billiard Sports Council of Hong Kong China
d. The Cycling Association of Hong Kong, China
e. The Equestrian Federation of Hong Kong, China
f. Hong Kong Fencing Association
g. The Gymnastics Association of Hong Kong, China
h. The Karatedo Federation of Hong Kong, China
i. Hong Kong, China Rowing Association
j. Hong Kong China Rugby
k. Sailing Federation of Hong Kong, China
l. Hong Kong China Skating Union

m. Squash Association of Hong Kong, China
n. Hong Kong China Swimming Association
o. Hong Kong, China Table Tennis Association
p. Hong Kong, China Tennis Association
q. Hong Kong, China Tenpin Bowling Congress
r. Triathlon Association of Hong Kong China
s. Windsurfing Association of Hong Kong, China
t. Hong Kong, China Wushu Union

302. Tier B Sports Associations include the following:

a. Hong Kong, China Contract Bridge Association
b. DanceSport Association of Hong Kong, China
c. Hong Kong China Dragon Boat Association
d. Golf Association of Hong Kong, China
e. The Judo Association of Hong Kong, China
f. Karting Association of Hong Kong, China
g. Lawn Bowls Association of Hong Kong, China
h. Hong Kong China Life Saving Society
i. Hong Kong, China Mountaineering and Climbing Union
j. Orienteering Association of Hong Kong, China
k. Hong Kong China Federation of Roller Sports and Skateboarding
l. Shuttlecock Association of Hong Kong, China
m. Hong Kong, China Taekwondo Association

HKSI

303. The HKSI provides elite sports training on behalf of the Hong Kong Government. It aims to be the leader in delivering elite training systems in the region, providing modern and evidenced-based sports training and support systems to identify, support and develop high-potential athletes. These athletes join the HKSI through recommendations from the relevant NSA, with the aim of progressing from Potential Athletes to Junior Athletes, then Elite Athletes. In addition to elite training facilities, the HKSI provides athletes with support such as scholarship schemes, sports science and medicine services, and education and personal development. The six centers in the Elite Training Science & Technology Division work to identify the different training issues and concerns and develop evidence-based solutions with the coaches.

304. Sports supported by the HKSI are classified into three tiers (Tier A*, Tier A and Tier B) under the Government's Elite Vote Support Scheme (EVSS). The EVSS assesses the achievements of athletes in various sports at major international competitions every two years. This pinpoints high-performing sports, which are supported by the HKSI for a four-year period (that aligns with Asian and Olympic Games cycles). The extent of funding and support varies based on the sport's classification.

305. Tier A* sports are Tier A sports whose athletes consistently excel at the elite international level and have the potential to obtain Olympic medals. They receive additional resources for enhanced training programs.

306. There are 6 Tier A* sports: Badminton, Cycling, Fencing, Swimming, Table Tennis, and Windsurfing.

307. Tier A sports are sports with an EVSS score of at least 10 points, whose Sports completed/will compete in at least three editions in the past four and upcoming two editions of the Olympic Games or Asian Games.

308. There are fourteen Tier A sports: Athletics, Billiards, Equestrian (i.e., horse riding), Gymnastics, Karatedo, Rowing, Rugby Sevens, Sailing, Skating, Squash, Tennis, Tenpin Bowling, Triathlon, and Wushu.

309. Tier B Sports are non-Asian and Olympic Games sports with an EVSS score between 7.5 and 10 points. Funding and support for Tier B sports are determined with the relevant NSAs and vary based on individual situations.

310. There are thirteen Tier B sports: Contract Bridge, Dance, Dragon Boat, Golf, Judo, Kart, Lawn Bowls, Life Saving, Mountaineering, Orienteering, Roller Sports, Shuttlecock, and Taekwondo.

311. There are two tiers of para-sport (Tier A and Tier B) to be supported for a four-year period by the HKSI under the EVSS system. The performance of para-athletes is assessed every two years, which aligns with the Asian Para and Paralympic Games cycle. The extent of funding and support also varies depending on the para sport's classification.

312. Tier A para sports encompass para sports with an EVSS score of at least 4 points. Para sports are required to have been competed/be competed in the past one or upcoming one edition of the Paralympic Games.

313. There are six Tier A para-sports, including Para-Badminton (Physical Disability), Boccia (Physical Disability), Para-Table Tennis (Physical Disability), Wheelchair Fencing (Physical Disability), Para-Swimming (Intellectual Disability), and Para-Table Tennis (Intellectual Disability).

314. Tier B para-sports are para-sports with an EVSS score of at least 3 points. Para-sports are required to have been competed/be competed in the past one or upcoming one edition of the Paralympic Games or Asian Para Games. The degree of funding and support is also determined through liaising with the relevant NSA and varies based on individual situations.

315. There are three Tier B para-sports, including Para-Athletics (Intellectual Disability), Para-Lawn Bowls (Physical Disability), and Para-Tenpin Bowling (Physical Disability).

316. For team sports, the HKSI provides further funding to eight Asian Games/ Asian Winter Games teams (with team sizes of at least five) to enhance the training programs of the Hong Kong representative teams, namely, Baseball, Basketball, Handball, Hockey, Ice Hockey, Softball, Volleyball and Water polo.

I. Main Regulations

317. Each of the above associations has its own constitutional document to govern the operation of the association.

318. The SF&OC also published different guidelines and rules including but not limited to the Anti-Doping Rules, Policy and Guidelines on Prevention of Sexual Harassment, and Child Safeguarding Policy 2022.

Part III. Sports and Employment

Introduction

319. The Basic Law of Hong Kong, which is the constitutional document of the HKSAR of the PRC, provides the following constitutional frameworks for Hong Kong employment law:

a. Article 33: Hong Kong residents shall have freedom of choice of occupation.
b. Article 39: The provisions of the International Covenant on Civil and Political Rights, the International Covenant on Economic, Social and Cultural Rights, and international labour conventions as applied to Hong Kong shall remain in force and shall be implemented through the laws of the Hong Kong Special Administrative Region.
c. Article 147: The Hong Kong Special Administrative Region shall on its own formulate laws and policies relating to labour.

320. Employment relationship in Hong Kong is predominantly governed by the EO (Cap. 57). Generally speaking, such relationships are also subject to various other ordinances, including but not limited to the:

a. Sex Discrimination Ordinance (Cap. 480);
b. Disability Discrimination Ordinance (Cap. 487);
c. Race Discrimination Ordinance (Cap. 602);
d. Family Status Discrimination Ordinance (Cap. 527);
e. Immigration Ordinance (Cap. 115);
f. Employees' Compensation Ordinance (Cap. 282);
g. Minimum Wage Ordinance (Cap. 608);
h. Occupational Safety and Health Ordinance (Cap. 509);
i. Factories and Industrial Undertakings Ordinance (Cap. 59);
j. PDPO (Cap. 486);
k. IRO (Cap. 112);
l. Mandatory Provident Fund Schemes Ordinance (Cap. 485); and
m. Trade Unions Ordinance (Cap. 332).

321. General Hong Kong employment law applies to the sports industry, despite there not being any statutory provisions that specifically apply to employment in the sports industry. Employers in the sports industry should ensure that they are in compliance with all these applicable laws and regulations.

§1. Sources of Employment Law

Applicability of the EO

322. In Hong Kong, a contract of employment is an agreement on the employment conditions made between an employee and an employer. The employment agreement can generally be made in writing or even orally. It covers generally both local and foreign employees. If the terms of an employment contract offer less protection to the employee than the EO, the EO will take precedence. Therefore, any attempt to reduce employee rights through a contract will be invalid. Generally speaking, the EO applies to each contract of employment. However, it should be noted that the EO does not generally apply to:

a. a person who is a member of the family of the proprietor of the business in which he is employed and who dwells in the same dwelling as the proprietor;
b. an employee as defined in the Contracts for Employment Outside Hong Kong Ordinance (Cap. 78);
c. a person who is serving under a crew agreement within the meaning of the Merchant Shipping (Seafarers) Ordinance (Cap. 478), or on board a ship which is not registered in Hong Kong;
d. contracts of apprenticeship registered under the Apprenticeship Ordinance (Cap. 47) except to the extent provided in that Ordinance.[185]

323. These exceptions should not normally apply to employers in the sports industry.

I. Ordinary Law

Minimum Wage

324. The minimum wage in Hong Kong is governed by the Minimum Wage Ordinance. Currently, the minimum wage in Hong Kong is HKD 40 per hour.[186] Generally speaking, an employee shall be paid an amount no less than the total number of hours (including any part of an hour) worked by the employee in the wage period multiplied by the minimum hourly wage rate. [187]

185. Section 4 of the EO.
186. https://www.labour.gov.hk/eng/news/mwo.htm.
187. Section 8 of the Minimum Wage Ordinance.

325. However, the Minimum Wage Ordinance does not apply to a student intern or work experience student during a period of exempt student employment as defined in the Minimum Wage Ordinance. [188]

326. In addition, an employee who holds a valid Registration Card for People with Disabilities issued by the Central Registry for Rehabilitation established by the government and whose productivity in performing the work required under the contract of employment is affected by a disability may be subject to a lower minimum wage, provided that the relevant conditions are met. [189]

327. Recently, the Hong Kong Government has agreed to change the mechanism for the review of the minimum wage [190] such that going forward, the Hong Kong statutory minimum wage will be reviewed annually based on the following formula:

> CPI(A) inflation (subject to a lower bound of zero) + the SEP factor where the CPI(A) shall be subject to a lower bound of 0%, and the SEP factor shall mean (the growth rate of the real GDP in the latest year –the trend growth rate of the real GDP in the latest decade) x 20%. The SEP factor shall be subject to an upper bound of 1% and a lower bound of 0%;

Anti-discrimination Laws

328. The Sex Discrimination Ordinance, Race Discrimination Ordinance, Disability Discrimination Ordinance and Family Discrimination Ordinance protect employees on the grounds of the specific protected characteristics, such as sex, marital status, pregnancy, breastfeeding, race, family status, race, color, descent, national or ethnic origin in prescribed areas of activities.

329. Different from some other jurisdictions, sexual orientation, religious belief and age are not expressly stipulated to be protected characteristics, at least in the case of private employers, in Hong Kong.

330. Discrimination includes both direct and indirect discrimination. For example, in the context of the Sex Discrimination Ordinance, discrimination by a man against a woman is defined to mean if:

a. on the grounds of her sex, he treats her less favorably than he treats or would treat a man; or
b. he applies to her a requirement or condition which he applies or would apply equally to a man but:
    i. which is such that the proportion of women who can comply with it is considerably smaller than the proportion of men who can comply with it;

188. Sections 7(4) and (5) of the Minimum Wage Ordinance.
189. Section 9(1)(b) of the Minimum Wage Ordinance.
190. https://www.info.gov.hk/gia/general/202404/30/P2024043000265.htm.

ii. which he cannot show to be justifiable irrespective of the sex of the person to whom it is applied; and
iii. which is to her detriment because she cannot comply with it.[191]

331. Discrimination against a man by a woman is also prohibited.[192] Some defenses are provided for under these anti-discrimination ordinances.

332. Harassment is also prohibited when considering certain protected characteristics. For example, in the context of the Sex Discrimination Ordinance, a person is deemed to have sexually harassed a woman if:

a. the person:
   i. makes an unwelcome sexual advance, or an unwelcome request for sexual favors, to her; or
   ii. engages in other unwelcome conduct of a sexual nature in relation to her, in circumstances in which a reasonable person, having regard to all the circumstances, would have anticipated that she would be offended, humiliated or intimidated; or
b. the person, alone or together with other persons, engages in conduct of a sexual nature which creates a hostile or intimidating environment for her.[193]

333. Vilification is also prohibited on certain protected characteristics. For example, in the context of the Race Discrimination Ordinance, it is unlawful for a person, by any activity in public, to incite hatred toward, serious contempt for, or severe ridicule of, another person or members of a class of persons on the ground of the race of the person or members of the class of persons.[194]

334. The anti-discrimination ordinance also prohibits discrimination by way of victimization. In the context of the Sex Discrimination Ordinance, it is stipulated that a person (the "**discriminator**") discriminates against another person (the "**person victimized**") in any circumstances relevant to the purposes of any provision of the Sex Discrimination Ordinance if he treats the person victimized less favorably than in those circumstances he treats or would treat other persons, and does so by reason that the person victimized or any other person (the third person) has:

a. brought proceedings against the discriminator or any other person under the Ordinance;
b. given evidence or information in connection with proceedings brought by any person against the discriminator or any other person under the Ordinance;
c. otherwise done anything under or by reference to the Ordinance in relation to the discriminator or any other person; or

191. Section 5 of the Sex Discrimination Ordinance.
192. Section 6 of the Sex Discrimination Ordinance.
193. Section 2(5) of the Sex Discrimination Ordinance.
194. Section 45 of Race Discrimination Ordinance.

d. alleged that the discriminator or any other person has committed an act which (whether or not the allegation so states) would amount to a contravention of the Ordinance,

or by reason that the discriminator knows the person victimized or the third person, as the case may be, intends to do any of those things, or suspects the person victimized or the third person, as the case may be, has done, or intends to do, any of them.[195]

335. It should be noted that the Sex Discrimination Ordinance does not generally apply in relation to any sport, game or other activity of a competitive nature where the physical strength, stamina or physique of the average woman puts her at a disadvantage to the average man, or render unlawful any act related to the participation of a person as a competitor in events involving that activity which are confined to competitors of one sex.[196]

336. According to research carried out by the Equal Opportunities Commission[197] in 2020, 90% of the surveyed national sports associations in Hong Kong have an anti-sexual harassment policy and/or a code of conduct as of October 2020. The Equal Opportunities Commission also notes that 57% of the surveyed national sports associations require employees and coaches who will engage in work with underage persons to undergo a sexual conviction record check.

337. The Equal Opportunities Commission issued a document entitled Formulating Policy on Sexual Harassment in Sports Organizations,[198] which provides guidance to sports associations on how to formulate their anti-sexual harassment policy.

Salaries Tax

338. The current salaries tax rates[199] after allowable deductions and allowances in Hong Kong are as below:

Net Chargeable Income (HKD)	*Rate (%)*
First 50,000	2
The next 50,000	6
The next 50,000	10
The next 50,000	14

195. Section 9 of the Sex Discrimination Ordinance.
196. Section 50 of the Sex Discrimination Ordinance.
197. Report on the Formulation of Anti-Sexual Harassment Policy among NSA in Hong Kong 2020, Equal Opportunities Commission, https://www.eoc.org.hk/eoc/upload/ResearchReport/2021125143401215386.PDF.
198. Reference Materials: Formulating Policy on Sexual Harassment in Sports Organizations, Equal Opportunities Commission, https://www.eoc.org.hk/eoc/upload/20213301635161268631.pdf.
199. Salaries Tax Rates, Hong Kong Government, https://www.gov.hk/en/residents/taxes/taxfiling/taxrates/salariesrates.htm.

Net Chargeable Income (HKD)	*Rate (%)*
The remainder	17

339. This is subject to the cap of the standard rate being:

Net Chargeable Income (HKD)	*Rate*
First 5,000,000	15%
The remainder	16%

340. Employers in Hong Kong have a general obligation to keep payroll records.[200] Employers also have tax filing obligations on an annual basis, when a new employee is hired and upon termination of an employee.[201]

341. There is no general tax withholding obligation on the part of the employers, save in the case of certain employees who are about to leave Hong Kong for any period exceeding one month and who are not required in the course of their employment to leave Hong Kong at frequent intervals. Except with the consent in writing of the Commissioner of Inland Revenue or in the case of money paid to the Commissioner on the direction of the individual, the employer shall not make any payment of money or money's worth to or for the benefit of the individual for a period of one month from the date on which the employer notified the IRD of the employee's expected departure.[202]

Data Privacy

342. The PDPO equally applies to the context of employment, including data protection principles as follows:

a. Personal data shall only be collected for a lawful purpose directly related to a function or activity of the data user. The data collected should be necessary and adequate but not excessive.
b. Data users shall take all practicable steps to ensure that personal data is accurate and is not kept longer than is necessary for the fulfillment of the purpose for which the data is used.
c. Personal data shall not be used for any new purpose which is not or is unrelated to the original purpose when collecting the data, unless with the data subject's express and voluntary consent.
d. All practicable steps should be taken to protect the personal data they hold against unauthorized or accidental access, processing, erasure, loss or use.

200. Section 51C of the IRO.
201. Section 52 of the IRO.
202. Section 52 of the IRO.

e. Data users shall take all practicable steps to ensure openness of their personal data policies and practices, the kind of personal data held and the main purposes for holding it. In practice, employers will provide a personal information collection statement before collecting the personal data of the employees, and will also maintain a data privacy policy.
f. Data subjects should be given the right to request access to and correction of their own personal data.

343. The Office of the PCPD, Hong Kong has issued various guidelines and leaflets for employment purposes. For example, the issuing of the Compliance Guide for Employers and Human Resource Management Practitioners, which addresses personal data issues pertaining to prospective employees, current employees and former employees.

344. Employers in the sports industry should be particularly careful when handling the personal data of sports athletes, given that the photos and videos (which may potentially constitute personal data) and other personal data of the athletes will often be used or disclosed during promotion campaigns and/or news updates, etc.

Statutory Holiday

345. Employees are currently entitled to fourteen days of statutory holidays,[203] being:

a. Lunar New Year's Day or, if that day falls on a Sunday, then the fourth day of Lunar New Year;
b. the second day of Lunar New Year or, if that day falls on a Sunday, then the fourth day of Lunar New Year;
c. the third day of Lunar New Year or, if that day falls on a Sunday, then the fourth day of Lunar New Year;
d. Ching Ming Festival;
e. Labor Day, being the first day of May;
f. Tuen Ng Festival;
g. the day following the Chinese Mid-Autumn Festival or, if that day falls on a Sunday, then the second day following that Festival;
h. the Chung Yeung Festival;
i. the Chinese Winter Solstice Festival or Christmas Day, at the option of the employer;
j. the first day of January;
k. HKSAR Establishment Day, being the first day of July;
l. National Day, being the first day of October;
m. the Birthday of the Buddha, being the eighth day of the fourth lunar month;
n. the first weekday after Christmas Day.

203. Section 39 of the EO.

346. The number of statutory holidays will be increased[204] in accordance with the following schedule:

Effective Year	*Additional Statutory Holiday*
2026	Easter Monday
2028	Good Friday
2030	The day following Good Friday

347. Generally speaking, an employee who has been employed by his employer under a continuous contract for a period of three months immediately preceding a statutory holiday shall be entitled to statutory holiday pay.[205]

348. As is the case of some other statutory payments, such as annual leave pay, paternity leave pay, maternity leave pay and statutory sickness allowance, the amount of statutory holiday pay is based on the concept of "wages." Generally speaking, the amount payable shall be the average daily wages of the relevant employees in the previous twelve months.[206]

349. "Wages" is technically defined under section 2(1) of the EO to mean, subject to subsections 2(2) and (3) of the EO:

> "all remuneration, earnings, allowances including travelling allowances and attendance allowances, attendance bonus, commission, overtime pay, tips and service charges, however designated or calculated, capable of being expressed in terms of money, payable to an employee in respect of work done or to be done under his contract of employment, but does not include—
>
> (a) the value of any accommodation, education, food, fuel, light, medical care or water provided by the employer;
> (b) any contribution paid by the employer on his own account to any retirement scheme;
> (c) any commission which is of a gratuitous nature or which is payable only at the discretion of the employer;
> (ca) any attendance allowance or attendance bonus which is of a gratuitous nature or which is payable only at the discretion of the employer;
> (cb) any travelling allowance which is of a non-recurrent nature;
> (cc) any travelling allowance payable to the employee to defray actual expenses incurred by him by the nature of his employment;
> (cd) the value of any travelling concession;
> (d) any sum payable to the employee to defray special expenses incurred by him by the nature of his employment;

204. Employment (Amendment) Ordinance 2021.
205. Section 40 of the EO.
206. Section 41 of the EO.

(da) any end of year payment, or any proportion thereof, which is payable under Part IIA;
(e) any gratuity payable on completion or termination of a contract of employment; or
(f) any annual bonus, or any proportion thereof, which is of a gratuitous nature or which is payable only at the discretion of the employer ... "

350. In practice, there are a number of disputes over whether a particular payment constitutes the wages of an employee or not. Given that the amount of wages would affect various statutory entitlements of employees, this is an issue that should be carefully considered. For example, if an employee is contractually entitled to an award upon winning in a competition, it is arguable that such an amount constitutes his wages and needs to be reflected in the amount of statutory holiday pay, annual leave pay, paternity leave pay, maternity leave pay and statutory sickness allowance.

351. If an event during which the employee has to work takes place on a rest day, there is no requirement to provide additional payment. However, an alternative holiday or substituted holiday should be granted.

352. An employer may grant an alternative holiday within the period of sixty days immediately preceding or next following the statutory holiday, provided that the employer has notified the employee, either orally or in writing or by notice posted in a conspicuous place in the place of employment, of the day on which he will be granted the alternative holiday: -

a. where the alternative holiday is to be taken on a day within the period of sixty days immediately preceding the statutory holiday, not less than forty-eight hours before that day; or
b. where the alternative holiday is to be taken on a day within the period of sixty days next following the statutory holiday, not less than forty-eight hours before the statutory holiday.[207]

353. In addition, the employer and the employee may agree that another day shall be substituted for a statutory holiday or an alternative holiday if such substituted holiday falls within the period of thirty days of such statutory holiday or alternative holiday.[208]

354. Employers in the sports industry should ensure the abovementioned requirements are complied with, especially if, for example, a statutory holiday happens to be on an event day that requires employees to work.

---

207. Section 39(2) of the EO.
208. Section 39(3) of the EO.

Working Hours

355. As of September 19, 2024, working hours are not generally regulated under the current Hong Kong legal framework.

356. Pursuant to the Employment of Young Persons (Industry) Regulations (Cap. 57C), the working hours of young persons at industrial undertakings are protected under the legislation.[209]

357. This does not mean that the employer can require employees to work excessive hours without limitation. This is because employers have, among other things, the obligation to ensure so far as reasonably practicable, the safety and health of their employees at work.[210]

Timing of Payment of Wages

358. Under the EO, wages shall become due on the expiry of the last day of the wage period (which shall, unless the contrary is provided, be deemed to be one month [211]) and shall be paid as soon as is practicable but in any case not later than seven days thereafter. [212]

Employees' Compensation Insurance

359. Under the Employees' Compensation Ordinance, no employer shall employ any employee in any employment unless there is in force an employees' compensation insurance that covers all relevant liabilities for injuries at work. [213] This is a special form of insurance and is different from general medical insurance. Employers should make sure to report to the insurers the place(s) of employment of the relevant employees.

360. Currently, the amount of required coverage [214] is as below:

Number of Employees	*Coverage per Event*
Does not exceed 200	HKD 100 million per event
Exceeds 200	HKD 200 million per event

209. For completeness, employment of children is regulated under the Employment of Children Regulations (Cap. 57B).
210. Section 6 of the Occupational Safety and Health Ordinance (Cap. 509).
211. Section 22 of the EO.
212. Section 23 of the EO.
213. Section 40 of the Employees' Compensation Ordinance.
214. Fourth schedule of the Employees' Compensation Ordinance.

§2. Employment Relationship

I. Employment Agreements

Continuous Contract

361. "Continuous contract" is an important concept underpinning the EO.

362. In essence, subject to some exceptions, an employee will be regarded as being employed under a continuous contract if the employee has been employed by the same employer for four consecutive weeks or more, during which he has worked for eighteen hours or more each week.[215]

363. The Hong Kong Government has proposed to revise the definition of "continuous contract" by using the aggregate working hours of four weeks as a counting unit and setting the four-week working hour threshold at sixty-eight hours.[216] It remains to be seen whether the proposal will be adopted by the Hong Kong LegCo.

364. The concept of continuous contract is important because many benefits under the EO may only be enjoyed by an employee who is employed under a continuous contract of employment for a specific period of time.

365. For example, employees who are not engaged under a continuous contract of employment will not be entitled to benefits such as paid statutory holidays, statutory severance payment, statutory long service payment, paid maternity leave, paid paternity leave, statutory sickness allowance or rest day.

366. In any dispute as to whether a contract of employment is a continuous contract, the onus of proving that it is not a continuous contract shall be on the employer.[217]

Fixed-Term Contracts

367. Fixed-term contracts are frequently used between football clubs and football players in Hong Kong. Fixed-term contracts, end on a specific date or upon task completion, are used in Hong Kong. The non-renewal of a fixed-term contract upon expiry is treated as a dismissal when determining statutory severance or long service pay. This does not preclude an employee from being engaged under a continuous contract under the EO.

Part-Time Workers

368. It is also popular for a sportsperson to be employed on a part-time basis. Under the EO, there is no distinction between part-time and full-time workers, except concerning the distinction between workers under a "continuous contract."

---

215. Schedule 1 to the EO.
216. Review of the "Continuous Contract" Requirement under the EO, LegCo of Hong Kong (Mar. 25, 2024), https://www.legco.gov.hk/yr2024/english/panels/mp/papers/mp20240325cb2-342-3-e.pdf.
217. Section 3(2) of the EO.

369. Some part-time employees and casual workers may not be able to meet the threshold of continuous contract, and hence they may be unable to enjoy most of the benefits under the EO. There are no other statutory provisions that confer special rights on part-time employees.

Employees and Independent Contractors

370. In Hong Kong, workers (including sportspersons) can engage with a business in two primary ways:

1. As an employee under a contract of employment (also known as a contract of service).
2. As an IC under an IC arrangement, such as a consultancy agreement, freelance contract, or contract for services.

371. The employment agreement may contain both implied and expressed terms, including the terms implied from the EO, common law and other relevant employment laws.

372. Employees, including sportspersons, are free to negotiate with the employers the terms and conditions of employment, provided that they do not violate the provisions of the EO and other relevant laws which aim to provide minimum employment protection for the employees. Any term of an employment contract that purports to reduce any benefit, right or protection conferred upon the by the EO will be void. Under the EO, an employer must inform the employee of certain specific conditions of employment before that employment begins.

373. Whether an individual is an employee engaged under a contract of service or an IC engaged under a contract for service is frequently subject to dispute. This is a critical issue as it will affect whether a particular individual is entitled to the statutory protection and benefits afforded to employees. This will also determine whether the hirer will be vicariously liable for the acts and omissions of the individual and whether the parties would be subject to the implied duties that arise under a contract of employment.

374. The leading authority in Hong Kong is the Hong Kong Court of Final Appeal's (HKCFA) decision in the case of *Poon Chau Nam v. Yim Siu Cheung* (2007).[218] In *Poon Chau Nam*, it was held that the modern approach is to examine all the features of the relationship against the background of the indicia developed in the case law with a view to deciding whether, as a matter of overall impression, the relationship is one of employment, bearing in mind the purpose for which the question is asked.[219]

218. (2007) 10 HKCFAR 156.
219. Paragraph 18 *of Poon Chau Nam v. Yim Siu Cheung* (2007) 10 HKCFAR 156.

375. The factors that have been taken into account in the previous case law include:[220]

a. whether in the performance of that service the servant will be subject to the other's control in a sufficient degree to make that other master;
b. whether the master has the right to control the method of doing the work;
c. whether the master has the power to select his servant;
d. whether in consideration of a wage or other remuneration, the servant will provide his own work and skill in the performance of some service for his master;
e. whether the master has the right of suspension or dismissal;
f. matter of economic reality, including the degrees of control, opportunities of profit or loss, investment in facilities, permanency of relation and skill required in the claimed independent operation;
g. whether the relevant individual is in business on his own account, including whether the man performing the services provides his own equipment, whether he hires his own helpers, what degree of financial risk he takes, what degree of responsibility for investment and management he has and whether and how far he has an opportunity of profiting from sound management in the performance of his task; and
h. whether the other provisions of the contract are consistent with its being a contract of service.

376. Additionally, how the worker and the business view their relationship (whether as employment or an IC relationship) may also be considered. However, this perception is not decisive; courts have from time to time determined a worker to be an employee despite the parties believing otherwise.

Immigration

377. Before the commencement of employment with an employee in Hong Kong, the employer shall ensure the employee has the right to work for the employer in Hong Kong.[221] No person shall in Hong Kong enter into a contract of employment to employ any other person unless he first inspects the identity card, valid travel document, official passport, etc., held by such other person.[222] Typically, the employing company sponsors the employment visa and must ensure the employee's repatriation when their stay ends. Employers must try to hire locally before seeking foreign workers (this requirement is less restrictive on hiring sportspersons from overseas), although there is no requirement for a certain percentage of employees or payroll to be local.

378. One must consider that some types of visas only allow the employee to work for a specific employer. If such employees have to work for an alternative

220. Paragraphs 11 to 17 of *Poon Chau Nam v. Yim Siu Cheung* (2007) 10 HKCFAR 156.
221. Section 17I of the EO.
222. Section 17J of the EO.

employer, it would be necessary for a change of sponsorship application to be submitted to the Immigration Department.

379. Currently, a person entering Hong Kong shall not take any employment, whether paid or unpaid or establish or join in any business. The Immigration Department, however, currently allows a visitor to generally engage in the following business-related activities:

a. concluding contracts or submitting tenders;
b. examining or supervising the installation/packaging of goods or equipment;
c. participating in exhibitions or trade fairs (except selling goods or supplying services directly to the general public, or constructing exhibition booths);
d. settling compensation or other civil proceedings;
e. participating in product orientation;
f. attending short-term seminars or other business meetings;
g. delivering speeches and presentations subject to certain conditions.[223]

380. The government has established an Immigration Facilitation Scheme. The purpose of the scheme is to provide immigration facilitation to visitors invited/sponsored by authorized host organizations for undertaking specified short-term activities for up to fourteen consecutive calendar days upon each arrival in Hong Kong, such that they will not need to apply for an employment visa/entry permit. Eligible visitors should be endorsed by the authorized host organizations by way of invitation letters.[224]

381. The scheme includes the sector of sports and covers athletes, coaches, visiting sports professionals, speakers and officiating guests and their accompanying supporting personnel participating in sports, conferences, ceremonies, seminars, workshops, training, exchanges, competitions and all other events. This includes "M" Mark events, Major Local International Events, Major National Championships and Local International Events by authorized host organizations.[225]

382. If entering Hong Kong is inevitable for foreign individuals to participate in an event, a reminder should be sent from the relevant organizers to those foreign individuals to ensure all the applicable immigration law requirements are satisfied.

223. Permissible Activities for Visitors, Hong Kong Immigration Department, https://www.immd.gov.hk/eng/services/visas/permissible-activities.html.
224. Regularization and Expansion of Pilot Scheme on Immigration Facilitation for Visitors Participating in Short-term Activities in Designated Sectors, Hong Kong Government Information Department, https://www.info.gov.hk/gia/general/202405/30/P2024053000172.htm?fontSize=1.
225. Immigration Facilitation Scheme: Scope of Facilitation, Hong Kong Government, https://www.immd.gov.hk/pdf/stv_scope_of_facilitation(e).pdf.

II. Players' Obligations

Rest Days

383. In general, an employee who has been employed by the same employer under a continuous contract shall be granted not less than one rest day in every period of seven days. Such rest days shall be in addition to any statutory holidays.[226]

384. It is worth mentioning to the reader that an employer shall, before the commencement of every month, inform each employee orally or in writing of his rest days in that month, unless the rest days are appointed on fixed days in each period of seven days on a regular basis.[227]

385. The EO does not explicitly stipulate that a rest day requires compensation.

386. The arrangement for rest days would require careful consideration if, for example, working on a rest day during an event is unavoidable for the employee.

Annual Leave

387. In general, an employee who has been in employment under a continuous contract for not less than twelve months shall be entitled to seven to fourteen days of annual leave depending on his year of service:[228]

Year of Service	*Number of Annual Leave*
1	7
2	7
3	8
4	9
5	10
6	11
7	12
8	13
9 or above	14

388. Similar to the aforementioned case of statutory holidays, the amount of statutory annual leave pay should also generally be calculated based on the formula of the average daily wages of the employee in the previous twelve months.

226. Section 17 of the EO.
227. Section 18 of the EO.
228. Section 41AA of the EO.

Sickness Allowance

389. Provided that the other requirements under the EO are satisfied, an employee who has been employed under a continuous contract for a period of one month or more immediately preceding a sickness day is entitled to sickness allowance.[229]

390. Generally, employees can accrue 2 paid sickness days for each completed month of employment during the first 12 months of such employment and 4 paid sickness days for each such month thereafter, subject to a maximum of 120 paid sickness days.[230]

391. In addition to having sufficient number of sickness days entitlement, employees have to take a sufficient number of consecutive days as sickness days before sickness allowance will be payable. Specifically, an employee shall take at least four consecutive days as sickness days,[231] except in the case of a female employee who is pregnant or who has given birth to a child and is required to attend a medical examination in relation to her pregnancy or post confinement medical treatment, or a female employee who is absent from work by reason of miscarriage.[232]

392. The relevant sickness days shall be supported by an appropriate medical certificate or a certificate of attendance.[233]

393. As is the case of some other statutory payments, such as annual leave pay, paternity leave pay, maternity leave pay and statutory holiday pay, the amount of statutory sickness allowance is based on the concept of "wages." In general, the amount payable for sickness allowance shall be 80% of the average daily wages of the relevant employees in the previous twelve months.[234]

394. It is important to note that other than in the case of summary dismissal, it is unlawful for an employer to terminate an employee on any sickness day taken by the employee in respect of which sickness allowance is payable.[235]

Maternity Leave

395. Generally speaking, an employee under a continuous contract shall be entitled to maternity leave[236] in the amount of:

229. Section 33(1) of the EO.
230. Section 33(2) of the EO.
231. Section 33(3) of the EO.
232. Sections 33(3A), (3B) and (3C) of the EO.
233. Sections 33(5B) and (6) of the EO.
234. Section 35 of the EO.
235. Section 33(4B) of the EO.
236. Sections 11(1) and (2) of the EO.

a. a continuous period of fourteen weeks;
b. a further period equal to the number of days, if any, beginning on the day after the expected date of confinement up to and including the actual date of confinement; and
c. a further period, not exceeding four weeks, on grounds of illness or disability arising out of the pregnancy or confinement.

396. With the agreement of her employer, a pregnant employee may decide on the date of commencement of her maternity leave, provided that such date is within a period of not less than two weeks before, and not more than four weeks before, the expected date of confinement.[237]

397. Provided that the appropriate procedural requirements are complied with, an employee who has been employed under a continuous contract for a period of not less than forty weeks immediately before the date of commencement of maternity leave shall be entitled to fourteen weeks' paid maternity leave.[238]

398. As is the case of some other statutory payments, such as annual leave pay, paternity leave pay, sickness allowance and statutory holiday pay, the amount of maternity leave pay is based on the concept of "wages." Generally speaking, the amount payable for sickness allowance shall be 80% of the average daily wages of the relevant employees in the previous twelve months.[239] The maximum amount of maternity leave pay payable for the eleventh to the fourteenth week of maternity leave shall be subject to a cap of HKD 80,000.[240]

399. It is important to note that other than in the case of summary dismissal, it is unlawful for an employer to terminate the employment of a pregnant woman who has served a notice of pregnancy from the date on which her pregnancy is confirmed by a medical certificate to the date on which she is due to return to work on the expiry of her maternity leave or the date of cessation of pregnancy (otherwise than by reason of confinement). An employer has to withdraw the notice of termination if a pregnant employee serves such a notice immediately after being informed of her termination of employment.[241]

Paternity Leave

400. Generally speaking, an employee under a continuous contract shall be entitled to five days of paternity leave.[242] Such paternity leave may be taken four weeks before the expected date of the delivery of the child and fourteen weeks beginning on the actual date of the delivery of the child.[243]

237. Section 12AA of the EO.
238. Section 14(2) of the EO.
239. Section 14(3A) of the EO.
240. Section 14(3E) of the EO.
241. Section 15 of the EO.
242. Section 15E of the EO.
243. Section 15E(3) of the EO.

401. Provided that the appropriate procedural requirements are complied with, an employee who has been employed under a continuous contract for a period of not less than forty weeks immediately before the date of commencement of paternity leave shall be entitled to five days of paid paternity leave.[244]

402. As is the case of some other statutory payments, such as annual leave pay, maternity leave pay, sickness allowance and statutory holiday pay, the amount of paternity leave pay is based on the concept of "wages." Generally speaking, the amount payable for sickness allowance shall be 80% of the average daily wages of the relevant employees in the previous twelve months.[245]

Severance Payment

403. Generally speaking, where an employee who has been employed under a continuous contract for a period of not less than two years is dismissed (including where the employee's fixed term contract is not renewed by the employer[246]) by reason of redundancy or is laid off, he shall be entitled to a statutory severance payment.[247]

404. The amount of severance payment shall generally speaking be:

a. in the case of a monthly rated employee, two-thirds of his last full month's wages, or two-thirds of HKD 22,500, whichever is less; and
b. in any other case, eighteen days' wages based on any eighteen days chosen by the employee and occurring during his last thirty normal working days, or two-thirds of HKD 22,500, whichever is less, for every year (and pro rata with respect to an incomplete year) of employment subject to a cap of HKD 390,000.[248]

405. It should be noted that, currently, employers in Hong Kong have the right to use the current accrued amount of the employer's portion of the Mandatory Provident Fund contribution to offset the liability to make such a severance payment.[249] Such offsetting right will be abolished in respect of a portion of statutory severance payment in respect of the period commencing May 1, 2025.[250] However, the government will implement a subsidy scheme whereby the government will, subject to certain conditions, subsidize part of the liability to make such severance payment.[251]

244. Section 15H of the EO.
245. Section 15I of the EO.
246. Section 31D of the EO.
247. Section 31B of the EO.
248. Section 31G of the EO.
249. Section 31I of the EO.
250. The Employment and Retirement Schemes Legislation (Offsetting Arrangement) (Amendment) Ordinance 2022.
251. Subsidy Scheme for Abolition of MPF Offsetting Arrangement, Hong Kong Labour Department, https://www.op.labour.gov.hk/en/government-scheme.html.

Long Service Payment

406. Generally speaking, where an employee who has been employed under a continuous contract for a period of not less than five years (a) is dismissed (including where the employee's fixed term contract is not renewed by the employer[252]) other than on the ground of redundancy or summary dismissal, (b) is certified as being permanently unfit for a particular type of work that he engages in, (c) terminates his contract and is not less than 65 years old, he shall be entitled to a long service payment, or (d) dies.[253]

407. The amount of long service payment shall generally speaking be:

a. in the case of a monthly rated employee, two-thirds of his last full month's wages, or two-thirds of HKD 22,500, whichever is less; and
b. in any other case, eighteen days' wages based on any eighteen days chosen by the employee and occurring during his last thirty normal working days, or two-thirds of HKD 22,500, whichever is less, for every year (and pro rata with respect to an incomplete year) of employment subject to a cap of HKD 390,000.[254]

408. It should be noted that currently, employers in Hong Kong have the right to use the current accrued amount of the employer's portion of the Mandatory Provident Fund contribution to offset the liability to make such a long service payment.[255] Such offsetting right will be abolished in respect of a portion of long service payment in respect of the period commencing May 1, 2025.[256] However, the government will implement a subsidy scheme whereby the government will, subject to certain conditions, subsidize part of the liability to make such long service payment.[257]

Mandatory Provident Fund contribution

409. Generally speaking, an employer shall register its regular employees who are between 18 and 65 years old into a Mandatory Provident Fund scheme and who have been employed for a continuous period of sixty days or more. Such registration shall be made within the first sixty days of employment.[258]

410. Not all of the employees are required to contribute to a Mandatory Provident Fund scheme.[259] For example, persons who enter Hong Kong under section 11

252. Section 31T of the EO.
253. Section 31R and 31RA of the EO.
254. Section 31V of the EO.
255. Section 31I of the EO.
256. The Employment and Retirement Schemes Legislation (Offsetting Arrangement) (Amendment) Ordinance 2022.
257. Subsidy Scheme for Abolition of MPF Offsetting Arrangement, Hong Kong Labour Department, https://www.op.labour.gov.hk/en/government-scheme.html.
258. Sections 7 and 7B of the Mandatory Provident Fund Schemes Ordinance.
259. Section 4 of the Mandatory Provident Fund Schemes Ordinance.

of the Immigration Ordinance for the purpose of employment (a) for not more than thirteen months or (b) who are members of a provident, pension, retirement or superannuation scheme of a place outside Hong Kong are not required to contribute to the Mandatory Provident Fund scheme.

411. Relevant employers and employees are required to contribute to the Mandatory Provident Fund scheme.[260] The current contribution requirements[261] are as below: -

Relevant Income in the Relevant Month	*Mandatory Contribution of the Employee*	*Mandatory Contribution of the Employer*
Less than HKD 7,100	N/A	5% of Relevant Income
HKD 7,100 to HKD 30,000	5% of Relevant Income	5% of Relevant Income
More than HKD 30,000	HKD 1,500	HKD 1,500

412. For this purpose, Relevant Income shall mean any wages, salary, leave pay, fee, commission, bonus, gratuity, perquisite or allowance, expressed in monetary terms, paid or payable by an employer (directly or indirectly) to that relevant employee in consideration of his employment under that contract, but does not include severance payments or long service payments under the EO.[262]

III. Termination Contract

Notice period

413. The EO regulates the notice period of employment contracts.

414. For an employment contract that has a probation period, a notice period is not required during the first month of the probation period.[263] For the remainder of the notice period, the notice period shall be the agreed period (if any) which shall not be less than seven days.[264]

415. If there is no probation period or subsequent to the completion of the probation period, the notice period for a continuous contract shall generally speaking be the agreed period (if any) which shall not be less than seven days. If there is no agreed period, the notice period shall be deemed to be one month.[265]

260. Section 7A of the Mandatory Provident Fund Schemes Ordinance.
261. MPF System Mandatory Contributions, Mandatory Provident Fund Schemes Authority, https://www.mpfa.org.hk/en/mpf-system/mandatory-contributions/employees#anchor1.
262. Section 2 of the Mandatory Provident Fund Schemes Ordinance.
263. Section 6(3) of the EO.
264. Section 6(3A) of the EO.
265. Section 6(2) of the EO.

416. Under the EO, both the employer and employee have the statutory right to make a payment in lieu of notice.[266]

Summary dismissal

417. Under the EO, an employer may summarily terminate an employee without notice or payment in lieu:

a. if the employee, in relation to his employment:
   i. willfully disobeys a lawful and reasonable order;
   ii. misconducts himself, such conduct being inconsistent with the due and faithful discharge of his duties;
   iii. is guilty of fraud or dishonesty; or
   iv. is habitually neglectful in his duties; or
b. on any other ground on which he would be entitled to terminate the contract without notice at common law.[267]

Termination without a valid reason

418. Unlike some other jurisdictions, the statute does not provide for a claim for "unfair dismissal" in Hong Kong. Part VIA of the EO contemplates a claim for unreasonable termination, or termination without valid reason for employees who have been employed under a continuous contract for not less than twenty-four months.

419. Under the EO, it shall be a valid reason to terminate an employee if the termination is by reason of:

a. the conduct of the employee;
b. the capability or qualifications of the employee for performing work of the kind that the employee was employed by the employer to do;
c. the redundancy of the employee or other genuine operational requirements of the business of the employer;
d. the fact that the employee or the employer or both of them would, in relation to the employment, be in contravention of the law, if the employee were to continue in the employment of the employer or, were to so continue without that variation of the terms of his contract of employment; or
e. any other reason of substance, which, in the opinion of the court or the Labor Tribunal, was sufficient cause to warrant the dismissal of the employee or the variation of the terms of that contract of employment.[268]

266. Section 7 of the EO.
267. Section 9 of the EO.
268. Section 32K of the EO.

420. However, it should be noted that the remedies for such a claim are generally regarded as limited. The Labor Tribunal may potentially order a pro-rated severance payment or long service payment if the employee does not otherwise meet the payment conditions for such severance payment or long service payment.

421. The Labor Tribunal has the power to grant additional remedies (for example, additional compensation) if the employee is terminated in contravention of certain prohibitions under statute (such as termination during maternity leave except as permitted under law) specified in the EO. If the employee's termination is in contravention of the specific prohibitions, the Labor Tribunal may make an order for reinstatement or re-engagement.[269]

Post-termination Restrictive Covenants

422. It is not uncommon for employers in Hong Kong to impose post-termination restrictive covenants restricting the activities of employees subsequent to the termination of employment.

423. The usual types of post-termination restrictive covenants include non-competition and non-solicitation clauses. Some of the employers may, for example, restrict the employees from joining another sports association after cessation of employment.

424. It should be noted that such post-termination restrictive covenants constitute a restraint of trade, and are prima facie void and unenforceable. However, if the employer can show that the restraints protect a legitimate interest, are in the interests of the parties and in the public interest, and are no more than reasonably necessary to protect the legitimate interests, the Court may uphold such restrictive covenants.

425. The reasonableness of the covenants would be assessed on a case-by-case basis. The factors that the Court would consider may include, among other things, the types of interests to be protected, duration of the restraint, geographical scope and nature of extent of activities to be restricted. Therefore, if employers in the sports industry would like to impose such restrictive covenants, they should carefully tailor the restrictive covenants to increase the likelihood that the restrictive covenants would be enforced by the Court.

§3. Agents' Regulations

Introduction

426. What is a sports agent?

269. Sections 32M to 32P of the EO.

"Sports Agent" is not legally defined in Hong Kong. In practice, a sports agent is essentially an intermediary who acts on behalf of professional athletes, managers/coaches and sports organizations in third-party negotiations. Depending on the terms of the agency agreement, the role of an agent can be all-encompassing and can involve anything from negotiating contracts to providing legal advice to professional athletes. Sports agents can act as the lynchpin between coaches, athletes, clubs and other sports institutions.[270]

427. One of the primary responsibilities of a sports agent is negotiating contracts. This usually involves negotiating terms of contracts including salaries of the athletes. Sports agents will invariably review market trends when dealing with offers and counteroffers on the athletes' behalf. Agents will also handle player contract extensions. Some agents also manage clients' finances including their tax matters. Agents are often involved in coordinating the careers of their clients and also helping them choose the clubs and institutions that suit them best. Sports agents also play an important role in the marketing and promotion of their clients including public relations events, coordinating interviews and public appearances for the athlete. Agents also scout the best talent in different sports.

428. In Hong Kong, as most sportsmen are amateur, the sports agents sector is less developed than those in Europe and North America. In fact, the only "professional sports" in Hong Kong are Football (the premier league organized by the HKFA) and Horse racing organized by the HKJC. That said, the Hong Kong Government has been providing support to some sportspersons allowing them to play sports on a full-time basis. In Hong Kong, the government, through the HKSI[271] provides support to eligible elite sports under the EVSS.[272] At the time of writing, there are twenty "Tier A" high-performance sports at the HKSI, including badminton, cycling, fencing, swimming, table tennis, windsurfing, athletics, billiard sports, equestrian, gymnastics, karatedo, rowing, rugby sevens, sailing, skating, squash, tennis, tenpin bowling, triathlon and wushu.

429. The concept of sport constituting an economic activity was first considered by the European Court of Justice in the case of *Walrave v. Union Cycliste.*[273] Since then, Sport has become a global industry. Like other industries in the new economic age, the sports industry is growing and evolving. The laws governing the sports industry are becoming more complex and difficult to understand and apply. Careful attention to valuable rights, present contingent and future rights and liabilities, and securing valuable interests are now necessary.

---

270. "Sports Agent Definition" (Law insider) https://www.lawinsider.com/dictionary/sports-agent.
271. The Hong Kong Sports Institute (Chinese: 香港體育學院) https://hksi.org.hk/ is a statutory sports institute mandated to provide training to athletes, and also offers academic qualification in the field of sports training.
272. "Tier A & B Sports," Hong Kong Sports Institute, https://www.hksi.org.hk/support-to-sports/tier-a-tier-b-sports (accessed Sep. 26, 2024).
273. Case 36/74 *Walrave and Koch* (1974) ECR-01405.

430. There is no separate legislative regime governing the law of sports agency in Hong Kong. In other words, general Hong Kong agency law applies to sports agents.

I. Regulations

431. There is no separate legislative regime governing the law of sports agency in Hong Kong. In other words, general Hong Kong agency law applies to sports agents.

432. Hong Kong agency law follows that of English Law which is governed by common law principles.[274] These principles govern the relationship between a principal and an agent and third parties and their respective rights and obligations. As such, Hong Kong agency law consists of a body of rules deriving from the law of contract and equity. Under the principle of freedom of contract, contracting parties are generally free to enter into contractual arrangements to agree on the terms of their relationship, including the scope of the agent's authority, commission, termination, governing law and jurisdiction. Hong Kong common law also governs the rights and liabilities of principals and agents. Many Hong Kong ordinances may also be relevant to agency principles and agency relationships and they are: Sale of Goods Ordinance (Cap. 26), Powers of Attorney Ordinance (Cap. 31), and Estate Agents Ordinance (Cap. 511) to name a few.

433. As explained, agency law deals with the relationships among the three parties namely the agent (in our case the Sports Agent), the principal (in our case the Athlete) and the third parties. An agent is an intermediary between the principal and third parties. A principal-agent relationship exists where one person has the authority or capacity to create legal relations between a person occupying the position of principal and third parties. A principal-agent relationship is created when the agent is given authority to act for the principal.

434. If in the exercise of his express or implied power given by the principal, a sports agent enters into a contract with a third party and expressly states that he is acting for and on behalf of a principal, the sports agent will then create a binding contract between the principal and that third party. The word agency may also be used to describe the situation where a person is appointed by another to act on his behalf.

274. "Nature and Formation of Agency." Essay. In Halsbury's Laws of Hong Kong, 15, 15.001. LexisNexis, a division of Reed Elsevier (Greater China) Ltd, 2022.

II. Rights

Express Appointment

435. Like other agencies, a sports agency is formed by express appointment when the principal appoints the agent through an oral or written agreement. General Common Law Contract principles apply, where an agent may act for a reward or gratuitously. In most cases, agency can be created orally, except when appointing an agent to execute a deed, which requires a power of attorney.

Agency by Estoppel (Implied Appointment)

436. This type of agency arises when a representation is made by A to a third party that B is a sports agent, leading the third party to interact with B as A's sports agent. A cannot deny the agency if it would harm the third party financially. The authority of the agent in this situation is apparent, not actual.

Agency by Ratification

437. Subject to registration requirements for specific sports agents, when a principal approves an act done by someone as their agent without actual authority at the time, agency by ratification occurs. This only creates an agency for the ratified act, not future ones. The person ratifying must have had legal capacity at the time of the act and ratification.

438. The HKCFA clarifies in *Secretary for Justice v. Chan Chi Wan Stephen & Anor*[275] that no pre-existing legal relationship is required for an agency relationship to arise under section 9 of the POBO.

III. Obligations

Sports Agents Authority

439. The actual authority of a sports agent includes express and implied authority. Express authority is explicitly given by the principal, while implied authority is necessary for effective duties. The sports agent's actual authority is determined by the agreement, trade customs, and past dealings. Contracts made by the agent within their actual authority bind the principal.

440. The sports agent represents the principal to the third party and has the authority to do what the principal can do (which is often limited by the sports agent's scope of authority). When the sports agent concludes a contract with a third party, the contract, while made between the agent and the third party, is the principal's contract with the third party. The sports agent falls away from such contractual relationship, and only the principal or the third party can sue or be sued on the contract. The essential feature of a sports agency is that it vests in the sports agent the power to alter the principal's legal relations with a third party.

275. (2017) 20 HKCFAR 98.

Apparent or ostensible authority

441. Apparent or ostensible authority refers to the situation where the principal has made a representation (whether by words or conduct) to the third party to the effect that the agent has the authority to act for him although the agent does not in fact have such authority; The third party has in fact relied on such representation to deal with the agent; and the third party has altered his position resulting from such reliance, for example, assuming obligations under a contract with the agent.

442. In essence, apparent or ostensible authority is authority which the principal induces a third party to believe the sports agent has when the sports agent in fact has not. The sports agent has only the appearance of authority, but no actual authority to act on behalf of the principal. Nevertheless, if the third party enters into a contract with the sports agent in reliance on the principal's representation, that contract will still be legally binding on the principal.

443. The principal's representation to the third party as to the authority of the sports agent to act on his behalf, when acted upon by that third party by entering into a contract with the sports agent, operates as an estoppel which prevents the principal from denying that such contract is binding upon him.

444. A Hong Kong sports agent has apparent authority when the principal leads a third party to believe the agent has authority, even if they do not. If the third party relies on this belief and enters a contract, it is binding on the principal. This creates an agency by estoppel, preventing the principal from denying the contract's validity. In the case of *Hong Kong v. Luk Kin Peter Joseph & Yu Oi Kee*,[276] the HKCFA clarified the scope of agency in the context of group companies for private sector offenses under the POBO.[277]

International versus Domestic Sports Rules

445. Sports law and the legal framework governing sports is a mix of general legal principles. In Hong Kong, the general legal principles concerning agency, employment, contract, tort, anti-competition, and copyright, etc., are applicable in the sports context. In the meantime, the international sports law, which is a separate and coherent set of rules, principles and procedures that specifically govern the conduct and consequences of international sports, may also be applicable to specific sports in Hong Kong.

International Sports Governing Bodies

446. At the international level, there is invariably an international federation governing a sport. For example, football (or soccer) is regulated by FIFA, which is the international self-regulatory governing body of association football.[278] FIFA was

276. [2016] HKCU 2964.
277. POBO, Cap. 201 Laws of Hong Kong.
278. https://www.fifa.com/en/member-associations/hong-kong.

founded to oversee international football competitions among the national associations. FIFA governs the sport of football through its statutes, rules, regulations and standing orders and the Law of the Game. FIFA controls football through a large number of committees including the Executive Committee, Emergency Committee, Finance Committee, Referee's Committee, Technical Committee, Sports Medical Committee, Players' Status Committee, Committee for Legal Matters, Committee for Security Matters and Fair Play, Media Committee, Protocol Committee, National Associations Committee, Doping Control Sub-Committee, Disciplinary Committee and Appeal Committee. Another example is the Olympic Games (also known as the Games of the Olympiad), which is a major international multi-sport event normally held once every four years, governed by the IOC, a non-governmental sports organization based in Lausanne, Switzerland.[279]

447. HKFA was established in 1914 as a Hong Kong company limited by guarantee.[280] The SF&OC, which was founded in 1950, is responsible for the participation of the Hong Kong Delegation to the Olympic Games, Asian Games and East Asian Games.[281] At present, there are altogether eighty-five member associations, i.e., NSA under SF&OC. HKFA and SF&OC are members of FIFA and the IOC, respectively. One can immediately see that notwithstanding that some sports are subject to domestic laws and regulations, the fact that the NSA are also members of international sports governing bodies makes international rules highly relevant in Hong Kong.

448. For instance, in 2023, the CAS,[282] which is an international arbitration institution for sports headquartered in Lausanne, Switzerland with an aim to facilitate the resolution of disputes in the field of sport, handed down an important ruling [283] that fully confirms the legality, validity and proportionality of the FIFA Football Agent Regulation (FFAR). The FFAR is a key development in FIFA's reform of the football transfer system, within its strategic goal of modernizing the football regulatory framework, and will regulate the work of football agents in the transfer of players. In November 2023, a prestigious arbitration tribunal in the U.K. ruled that key elements of FIFA's FFAR would, if implemented by the Football Association in the U.K., constitute an illegal agreement and an abuse of a dominant position in breach of U.K. competition law because the Fee Cap operated as an anti-competitive horizontal purchasing agreement on the part of football clubs, and that, if implemented, would amount to restrictions of competition.[284] Although this is an arbitral award in the U.K., it is persuasive in Hong Kong Courts in determining Hong Kong's own Competition Ordinance. This is also a good example of how rules under international sports organizations impact domestic legislations.

279. https://olympics.com/ioc/overview.
280. https://www.hkfa.com/en/about-us/organisation.
281. https://www.hkolympic.org/about-us/history/.
282. https://www.tas-cas.org/en/general-information/history-of-the-cas.html.
283. https://www.tas-cas.org/fileadmin/user_upload/CAS_Award_9370.pdf.
284. https://www.brickcourt.co.uk/images/uploads/documents/caa-v-fa-and-fifa-301123-.

§4. Trade Unions

449. Trade unions in Hong Kong are primarily governed by the Trade Unions Ordinance. Registered trade unions have certain rights and are mostly composed of employee unions, with some employers' associations and mixed organizations.

450. Employees are free to join these unions and are protected when participating in union activities. There is no legislation in Hong Kong that mandates collective bargaining, meaning agreements between unions and employers are not automatically binding. Strikes and trade disputes are relatively rare.

§5. Sports Dispute Resolution

International Sports Law and Dispute Resolution

451. As explained previously, the Hong Kong judiciary has experience in dealing with disputes within the sports sector. In addition, certain international sports organizations may also have their own rules for resolving disputes of a specific sport. Within the realm of international sports law, a significant focus is on sports dispute resolution, a field predominantly overseen by the CAS.[285] In brief, the growth of international sports over the past fifty years has seen a corresponding increase in sports-related disputes across various nations and regions. This necessitated the establishment of an independent and impartial authority specializing in sports disputes. Additionally, the inherently transient nature of sports demanded a swift resolution process. Consequently, the CAS was founded in 1984 and continues to be the preeminent international body for sports dispute resolution.

452. The primary role of CAS is to resolve legal disputes directly or indirectly related to sports through arbitration or mediation. These disputes can encompass issues such as contractual breaches, disciplinary matters, doping, athlete eligibility, and commercial disputes related to sponsorship and advertising.

453. The CAS operates under the Code of Sports-related Arbitration and comprises three divisions:

- Ordinary Arbitration Division: Handles disputes arising from contractual relations or torts.
- Appeals Arbitration Division: Deals with disputes stemming from decisions made by federations, associations, or other sports-related entities.
- Anti-Doping Division: Specializes in resolving anti-doping disputes.

454. Any Hong Kong individual or legal entity, including athletes, sports federations, clubs, event organizers, or sponsors, can invoke the jurisdiction of CAS,

285. History of the CAS, CAS, https://www.tas-cas.org/en/general-information/history-of-the-cas.html.

provided there is an agreement to submit disputes to CAS arbitration. Such agreements are typically embedded in contracts or the statutes and regulations of sports organizations. The arbitral awards issued by CAS are final and binding, enforceable under the New York Convention. Appeals to the Swiss Federal Court are limited to specific grounds such as lack of jurisdiction, procedural violations, or conflicts with public policy, similar to other arbitration proceedings.[286]

455. In addition to arbitration, CAS offers mediation services governed by its own mediation rules. The CAS mediation process is non-binding and aims to facilitate good faith negotiations and settlements, primarily for contractual disputes. Disciplinary disputes, like match-fixing and doping, are generally excluded unless exceptional circumstances and mutual consent allow. CAS mediation can occur even after the commencement of ordinary or appeal arbitration procedures. Moreover, a "Med/Arb" procedure is available, enabling parties to resort to arbitration if mediation fails to achieve a settlement.

456. While CAS provides both arbitration and mediation services, arbitration remains the predominant method for resolving sports disputes. This is evidenced by the current CAS roster of arbitrators. CAS has permanent decentralized offices in Sydney and New York, and alternative hearing centers in Abu Dhabi, Cairo, Kuala Lumpur, and Shanghai. Despite the hearing venue, the seat of arbitration for all CAS procedures remains in Lausanne, Switzerland. As of September 26, 2024, CAS lists 463 arbitrators and 52 mediators.[287]

Central People's Government and Hong Kong Government's strategy on Sports Dispute Resolution

457. Under the National 14th Five-Year Plan and the Outline Development Plan for the Guangdong-Hong Kong-Macao Greater Bay Area,[288] the Central People's Government has designated Hong Kong as a hub for international legal and dispute resolution services in the Asia-Pacific region. As the global sports industry expands rapidly, there's a growing need for specialized dispute resolution services to address various sports-related conflicts, such as competition issues, disciplinary matters, contractual disputes, and governance concerns. Establishing an effective sports dispute resolution mechanism is crucial to meet the needs of diverse stakeholders, including athletes, sports organizations, federations, event sponsors, and others.

458. To foster sports development in Hong Kong, having an efficient and robust mechanism for resolving sports-related disputes is essential. Delays in handling

---

286. "Frequently asked questions: Is it possible to appeal against a CAS award," Court of Arbitration for Sports, https://www.tas-cas.org/en/general-information/frequently-asked-questions.html#:~:text=Judicial%20recourse%20to%20the%20Swiss%20Federal%20Tribunal%20is,a%20fair%20hearing%29%20or%20incompatibility%20with%20public%20policy.%C2%AD%C2%AD%C2%AD (accessed on Sep. 26, 2024).
287. Lists of arbitrators (general lists), Court of Arbitration for Sports, https://www.tas-cas.org/en/arbitration/liste-des-arbitres-liste-generale.html (accessed on Sep. 26, 2024).
288. Outline Development Plan for the Guangdong-Hong Kong-Macao Greater Bay Area https://www.bayarea.gov.hk/filemanager/en/share/pdf/Outline_Development_Plan.pdf.

conflicts can significantly impact an athlete's career. Furthermore, developing sports dispute resolution capabilities would reinforce Hong Kong's status as a center for international legal and dispute resolution services in the Asia-Pacific region. Globally, various sports dispute resolution mechanisms with established rules and dedicated offices are in place. For instance, CAS is acknowledged as the leading international body for sports dispute resolution.

459. In Hong Kong, sports-related disputes arise, but there is no unified dispute-resolution mechanism within the sports sector. Local sports associations tend to resolve disputes through internal procedures, with only a few incorporating arbitration or mediation clauses in their constitutions or internal rules. There is a limited uptake of ADR for sports-related disputes in Hong Kong, which can be attributed to several factors:

- Absence of dispute resolution clauses in relevant constitutions, rules, and agreements.
- Lack of resources within sports associations.
- Preference for internal mechanisms.
- Lack of awareness about the benefits and procedures of ADR among potential users, such as local sports associations and athletes.

460. Hong Kong possesses unique strengths in offering sports dispute resolution services and supporting overall local sports development. The city has a comprehensive legal framework and a supportive judiciary that facilitates arbitration and mediation. The three reciprocal arbitration arrangements signed with Mainland China provide exceptional convenience for arbitration users in Hong Kong to resolve disputes involving Mainland-related elements. Additionally, Hong Kong has a strong pool of professionals experienced in sports dispute resolution. As of September 24, 2024, there are 102 arbitrators listed with the HKIAC, 96 arbitrators listed with AALCO-HKRAC and 145 mediators on the panel of the Hong Kong Mediation Accreditation Association Limited, all possessing expertise in sports.

Labor Dispute Resolution within the sports sector

461. The Hong Kong Labor Tribunal provides a swift, informal, and cost-effective means for resolving monetary disputes between employees and employers.[289] Legal representation is not permitted, requiring parties to present their cases independently. While Tribunal Officers can assist in drafting one's claim form and the Presiding Officer will aid during hearings, the Tribunal does not offer legal advice regarding claims. It is advisable to seek independent legal counsel if needed.

462. The Tribunal has specific jurisdiction and can handle the following types of claims:

- Monetary Claims Exceeding HKD 15,000.

289. Labour Tribunal Ordinance (Cap. 25).

- Statutory Non-Compliance Claims with the EO, the Minimum Wage Ordinance, or the Apprenticeship Ordinance.
- Claims involving breaches of employment contract terms, whether the contract is performed in Hong Kong or governed by the Contracts for Employment Outside Hong Kong Ordinance (Cap. 78).

463. Therefore, employees (including sportspersons) frequently lodge claims for the following:

- Unpaid wages for work performed.
- Wages in lieu of notice if an employer terminates a contract without the requisite notice.
- Payment for statutory holidays, annual leave, or rest days.
- Severance pay, long service payment, or terminal payments.
- End-of-year payment, double pay, or annual bonuses.
- Commission dues.

Part IV. Doping and Sports

§1. Legal Framework

I. Introduction

464. As a fair playing field is a tenet of sports games, the integrity of a game requires that players are not advantaged by the use of drugs. Doping in sports is a global issue. In recent years, there has been an increasing number of doping cases in sporting competitions. The total number of anti-doping rules violations reached 910 in 2020,[290] and more than half of these violations resulted in sanctions being imposed on the athlete.

465. In Hong Kong, there is a robust legal framework that is in line with international standards to fight against doping in sports. The Anti-Doping Organization of Hong Kong, China, formerly known as the Hong Kong Anti-Doping Committee (HKADC), is the official anti-doping independent organization in Hong Kong.[291] This organization operates under the World Anti-Doping Code, ensuring that Hong Kong's Anti-Doping Rules are in full compliance with international regulations. It aims to provide a comprehensive anti-doping framework to deter doping and uphold the principles of fair play in Hong Kong's sports sector.

II. Ordinary legislation

466. There is no legislation in Hong Kong targeting doping in sports specifically, but the process of doping may be covered by Hong Kong's criminal legislation. The sale, trafficking, and illegal import of drugs for doping may all be considered serious criminal offenses,[292] and the person engaging in these activities may risk prosecution in Hong Kong.

467. According to the Pharmacy and Poisons Ordinance (Cap. 138), the sale of unregistered pharmaceutical products, including some performance-enhancing

290. Sports doping worldwide—statistics & facts, Statista at https://www.statista.com/topics/9029/doping-in-professional-sports/, accessed on Aug. 16, 2024.
291. "About us" Anti-Doping Organization of Hong Kong, China, at https://www.antidoping.hk/about-us/background/ accessed on Aug. 16, 2024.
292. *Legal Implications of Trafficking Prohibited Substances*, published April 2023, Anti-Doping Organization of Hong Kong, China.

drugs, is a criminal offense punishable by a level 6 fine (i.e., HKD 100,000) and imprisonment of two years.[293] Most performance-enhancing drugs contain steroids, and in Hong Kong, pharmaceutical products containing steroids are all classed as poisons in the Pharmacy and Poisons Ordinance and can only be sold with a proper license.

468. If athletes import drugs into Hong Kong from overseas, such as drugs included in the WADA Prohibited List classes S6 stimulants, S7 narcotics and S8 cannabinoids, these athletes may be prosecuted for illegal trafficking of dangerous drugs under the Dangerous Drugs Ordinance (Cap. 134).[294] If convicted, the maximum penalty is a fine of HKD 5 million and life imprisonment.

469. The import of any pharmaceutical product into Hong Kong is under the strict control of the Department of Health. If athletes intend to import a certain pharmaceutical product into Hong Kong, a license must first be obtained from the Department of Health. This applies to all pharmaceutical products.

470. Therefore, athletes from jurisdictions that might allow the use and possession of drugs that are regulated in Hong Kong must be careful to respect the laws and not import them into Hong Kong, otherwise, they may be subject to arrest.

471. Distributing dangerous drugs in Hong Kong is also a serious offense, as the Dangerous Drugs Ordinance only allows dangerous drugs to be sold under the supervision of a registered pharmacist with a medical prescription.

472. The criminal laws in relation to the sale and import of the most common doping drugs used by athletes all apply to internet and black-market sales as well. Breaking these laws will not only result in athletes being barred from competing in sporting competitions but also result in them receiving criminal conviction(s) with possible prison sentences.

III. Sports Regulations

473. The Anti-Doping Organization of Hong Kong, China is the official anti-doping governing body in Hong Kong. Many Hong Kong sports clubs also follow the Anti-Doping Rules published by the Anti-Doping Organization of Hong Kong, China.

474. The Anti-Doping Organization of Hong Kong, China has a Prohibited List published on their website based on WADA: https://www.druginsport.hk/. This allows athletes to easily find out whether a specific drug is a poison or regulated drug in Hong Kong, preventing any possible trouble when bringing and using certain drugs in Hong Kong during competitions.

293. Pharmacy and Poisons Ordinance (Cap. 138).
294. Dangerous Drugs Ordinance (Cap. 134).

475. Apart from drugs explicitly stated on the Prohibited List, substances that meet certain criteria could also be included on the Prohibited List. Any substances or methods meeting the following criteria could be included on the Prohibited List if:

1. Two of these criteria are met:
   a. Potential to enhance sport performance.
   b. The use represents actual or potential health risk.
   c. The use violates the spirit of sport.
2. Potential to mask the use of other prohibited substances and prohibited methods.[295]

476. Enforcement of the Anti-Doping Rules in Hong Kong is also carried out by the Anti-Doping Organization of Hong Kong, China. The organization will regularly conduct testing and investigations as part of the anti-doping program.[296] It carries out both in-competition and out-of-competition testing of athlete's samples. The determination of which athlete to be selected for testing and when the testing will be done is based on a number of factors, such as their ranking, the type of sport engaged in, and the phase of the season of competitions of the sport.

477. If an athlete is found to have committed an Anti-Doping Rule violation, they may face sanctions. These can include disqualification of results, ineligibility for a specified period, and forfeiture of any medals, points, and prizes. The specific sanctions depend on the nature and severity of the violation, the athlete's degree of fault, and whether it is the athlete's first violation.

IV. Sports Courts

478. Unlike many other countries, Hong Kong does not currently have a court dedicated to resolving sports-related disputes. However, it does not mean that there are no set procedures for dealing with sports-related disputes in Hong Kong, including doping allegations.

479. It is important to note that internal procedures have been developed by local sports associations to resolve disputes, such as the procedure for doping incidents developed by the Anti-Doping Organization of Hong Kong, China.

480. When an athlete in Hong Kong has been found to have committed a doping violation, a hearing procedure will be triggered by the Hong Kong Anti-Doping Disciplinary Panel. The athlete will be notified of the potential consequences of the doping violation, and if the athlete wants to dispute the doping allegation, a hearing

295. Extracted from the webpage of Anti-Doping Organization of Hong Kong, China at https://www.antidoping.hk/substances-2/the-prohibited-list/, accessed on Aug. 18, 2024.
296. *Anti-Doping Rules of HKADC*, HKADC (Now Anti-Doping Organization of Hong Kong, China), published in January 2021.

can be requested. The Hong Kong Anti-Doping Disciplinary Panel will be conducting the hearing, and the athlete has the right to seek legal advice and present his/her case and evidence. After the hearing, the Panel will decide whether the evidence provided by the athlete is sufficient to acquit him/her. This decision will also decide whether and what sanctions will be imposed. After the Panel's decision, the athlete still has the right to appeal against the decision.

481. As there are no official legal procedures or court hierarchy for sports-related disciplinary actions and anti-doping violations in Hong Kong, there is a certain amount of difficulty for athletes to appeal against the decision of the Hong Kong Anti-Doping Disciplinary Panel. However, according to a LegCo Discussion Paper published by the Department of Justice,[297] Hong Kong possesses unique strengths in providing sports dispute resolution services in support of the overall local sports development. There is also a strong pool of legal professionals which has a wealth of experience in dealing with sports dispute resolution matters.[298] According to statistics provided in the LegCo Paper,[299] there are 99 arbitrators listed in HKIAC and 144 mediators on the panel of Hong Kong Mediation Accreditation Association Limited with expertise in sports matters.

482. Thus, arbitration can be the best legal procedure to resolve these sports-related disciplinary disputes. As a highly regarded forum for international arbitration, Hong Kong possesses an abundance of arbitration institutions to administer these sports-related arbitration cases, such as the AALCO-HKRAC and HKIAC. Arbitral awards are binding in nature, and decisions made through arbitration processes can serve as an effective deterrent against inappropriate or unethical behavior in sports. The furtherance of Hong Kong's sports arbitration mechanism in alignment with the CAS would undoubtedly enhance the ability of Hong Kong sports associations to enforce their internal rules and constitutions in a consistent manner, thereby contributing toward the preservation of the integrity and sportsmanship of the city's competing athletes and sporting events as well.

V. Case Law

483. Although there are yet to be cases on Hong Kong athletes violating the Anti-Doping Rules, there are some notable cases of Chinese athletes being found in violation of doping incidents, in which the cases have been escalated to the CAS, which is a globally recognized international arbitration center in Switzerland dedicated to resolving sports-related disputes.

484. In 2020, the CAS issued a ruling in the *Sun Yang doping* case, which is a high-profile case of a Chinese athlete violating anti-doping rules by using

297. *Development of Sports Dispute Resolution in Hong Kong*, LC Paper CB(4)642/2024(02), LegCo Discussion Paper.
298. *Ibid.*
299. *Ibid.*

performance-enhancing drugs.[300] The Chinese swimmer was held to have violated the rules and sanctioned with an eight-year period of ineligibility for intentionally interfering with a blood sample collection attempt, a violation of the WADA World Anti-Doping Code. Despite not being directly related to Hong Kong, this case highlights the use of arbitration to reach a binding decision in sports-related disciplinary disputes.

485. In the 2024 Paris Olympics, American gymnast Jordan Chiles finished the floor exercise with a score of 13.666, placing her 5th, with Romanian gymnast Ana Barbosu winning a bronze. Subsequent to the competition, Chiles' coach filed an inquiry relating to the score, which was accepted, resulting in Chiles being placed 3rd. The Romanian Gymnastics Federation appealed on behalf of the original bronze medalist, Ana Barbosu, and CAS determined the inquiry was filed out of time and reverted Chiles' score back to 13.666.[301] The bronze medal is awarded to Ana Barbosu, leading to Chiles' appeal. The CAS ruling was supported by the International Gymnastics Federation (FIG) and the IOC.[302] American gymnast Jordan Chiles then filed an appeal to Switzerland's Supreme Court against the CAS decision. The results remain to be seen.

300. Zubcic, L., Windholz, E. & Ng, YF. Smashed vials, fair trials? *Sun Yang* and procedural fairness at the CAS. *Int Sports Law J* 23, 176–197 (2023). https://doi.org/10.1007/s40318-023-00242-9.

301. Amari Apple, "Jordan Chiles appeals Olympic medal ruling" (Rollingout, September 2024) https://rollingout.com/2024/09/19/jordan-chiles-appeals-olympic-ruling/.

302. Ashless Buhler, "Romanian gymnast Ana Barbosu awarded bronze medal after CAS ruling" (NBC Olympics, August 2024), https://www.nbcolympics.com/news/romanian-gymnast-ana-barbosu-awarded-bronze-medal-after-cas-ruling.

Part V. Sport and Commerce

Introduction

486. Sports have the magical power of moving people to express their passion, unity and appreciation for human talent, teamwork and recognition of the hard work athletes have for training.

487. Sports, at their core, are arenas for competition, entertainment, and human achievement. However, behind the scenes, a multitude of commercial activities drive the industry forward. Athletes, teams, clubs, sponsors, and governing bodies engage in a complex web of transactions that shape the very fabric of the sports world. From the acquisition and disposal of professional clubs and teams to endorsement deals, the sports industry is a thriving marketplace where legal consideration is paramount.

488. Unless there are any special rules and regulations, sports-related transactions are also subject to general contract law. To establish a binding contract, there are four essential elements, which are (1) offer, (2) acceptance, (3) consideration, and (4) intention to create legal relations.

489. As with other common law jurisdictions, in Hong Kong, an "offer" is "an expression of willingness to contract on specified terms made with the intention that it is to become binding as soon as it is accepted by the person to whom it is addressed." [303] There is no contract unless the other party accepts the offer. Acceptance is a final and unqualified expression of assent to the terms of the offer.[304] To determine whether an agreement has been made, what its terms are and whether it is intended to be binding, an objective approach is adopted.[305]

490. Another important element is consideration. Consideration must be sufficient but need not be adequate. The fairness of the bargain is not a concern in law.

303. Beale, H.G. and Chitty, J. (2012a) *Chitty on contracts: Vol. 1: General principles*. 31st ed. London: Sweet & Maxwell.
304. *Ibid.*
305. *Cheung Ah Mei & Anor v. Wong Shiu Ling* [2020] HKCU 538.

491. Last but not least, the parties of a contract shall have a common intention to create legal relations between themselves. The basic question is "would a reasonable person conclude that the parties intended to make their agreement legally binding?" In ordinary commercial transactions, it is not normally necessary to prove the intention. The onus of proving that there was no such intention is on the party who asserts that no legal effect is intended.

492. Sports contracts with athletes typically fall into three main categories: professional services, endorsements, and appearances, all of which involve payment for services of the athlete's unique talents, abilities and skills. Additionally, business-related sporting activities such as media, sponsorship, and marketing are also considered commercial in nature. Therefore, as these sports-related agreements are usually commercial in nature, there is likely a presumption of intention to create legal relations.[306]

§1. Sponsorship

493. Sports sponsorship can be a win-win situation for both the sports-related parties and the brand involved. Sponsorships provide opportunities for brands to engage with a targeted audience that shares a common interest. By implementing a tailored sponsorship strategy, companies can expand the influence of their brands.

494. However, sponsorships can provide the necessary financial support for athletes and sports teams to continue performing and competing at a high level. This is especially important in cases where government funding for sports may be limited.

495. There are different types of sponsorships.

496. For example, the HKJC has an altruistic JCAIAS, which provides cash incentives to athletes with top results for three years to 2025.

497. Athlete sponsorship can also be effected through commercial endorsement deals. Companies may wish to have their brand connected or linked with famous athletes who align with their brand image. Under these arrangements, sponsors pay a fee to associate their brand with the athlete.

498. It is crucial to meticulously structure the terms of these contracts. Both parties involved should have a clear understanding of their obligations, especially those that are continuing in nature. We set out examples of important clauses which should be considered when parties enter such contracts.

---

306. *Esso Petroleum Ltd v. Comrs of Customs and Excise* [1976] 1 WLR 1.

499. Non-competition restrictive covenants may prohibit athletes from entering into similar endorsement agreements with rival competitors, to avoid brand dilution. To be enforceable, the restrictive covenant shall be reasonable[307] in terms of the duration of the restraint period and geographical restraint.

500. In addition to general legal considerations such as notice, liability and dispute resolution, disclaimers for various scenarios should also be reviewed. If such disclaimers exist, both parties should consider whether they are acceptable to them.

501. Termination clauses should be included to enable a clear way to terminate the contract, should unhappy differences arise.

502. Another form of sponsorship is team sponsorship, which involves sponsoring a professional, amateur, or collegiate team. In this type of sponsorship, the sponsor pays a fee to have their brand prominently displayed on team uniforms and equipment, etc. The cost of branding placements on uniforms and equipment can vary for different positions, sizes and the competition itself.

503. With the advancement of technology, brands can even sponsor posts on a team's social media accounts. In 2023, the Hong Kong Eastern Sports Club Football Team received a seven-figure sponsorship from XDAG Foundation.[308] The sponsorship included branding on the front of the team's jerseys and sponsored posts on selected social media platforms.

504. Sport sponsorships encompass more than just athletes, teams and event sponsorships, and can also extend to venue sponsorships.

505. Apart from the existing stadiums in Hong Kong, the upcoming Kai Tak Sports Park is set to be the largest-ever investment in the sports sector for the region. Anticipated to open in 2025, the construction cost of the sports park is estimated to reach tens of billions of dollars. This ambitious project showcases Hong Kong's commitment to developing world-class sports infrastructure and facilities.

506. Stadium financing lies at the crossroads of the entertainment business and the public interest. On one hand, the public's ever-growing appetite for sporting events over the years has spawned numerous colossal projects requiring financing packages similar to those for public or industrial infrastructure projects of the same scale. On the other, the economic benefits and social impact of projects of various

307. *Susan Buchanan v. Janesville* [1981] HKLR 700.
308. East receives 7-figure sponsorship from Cryptocurrency Foundation Vice Chairman: Proving the right direction will pay off (translated), Ming Pao, Aug. 10, 2023, https://news.mingpao.com/ins/%e9%ab%94%e8%82%b2/article/20230810/s00006/1691664226433/%e6%b8%af%e8%b6%85-%e6%9d%b1%e6%96%b9%e7%8d%b2%e5%8a%a0%e5%af%86%e8%b2%a8%e5%b9%a3%e5%9f%ba%e9%87%91%e6%9c%837%e4%bd%8d%e6%95%b8%e8%b4%8a%e5%8a%a9-%e5%89%af%e4%b8%bb%e5%b8%ad-%e8%ad%89%e6%98%8e%e6%96%b9%e5%90%91%e6%ad%a3%e7%a2%ba%e6%9c%83%e6%9c%89%e5%9b%9e%e5%a0%b1.

sizes often warrant the use of public funds, and the involvement of local communities may be imperative in the case of facilities where utility takes precedence over profitability.

507. In Hong Kong, the Public Finance Ordinance (Cap. 2) establishes the framework for the control and management of public finances. The members of LegCo are responsible for scrutinizing and approving the public expenditure proposals put forward by the government.

508. Negotiating sponsorship deals for stadium financing involves a strategic and collaborative process between the stadium owners/operators and potential sponsors. Similar to negotiations for sponsorship deals involving public spaces like schools and hospitals, the issue of naming rights takes center stage when it comes to negotiating sponsorship deals for stadium financing. If the stadium or arena is publicly owned rather than team-owned, obtaining approval from the Hong Kong government may be necessary for granting naming rights to the facility.

509. Since a naming right is a long-term right, the parties shall consider not only unfavorable contingencies but also the evolving nature of naming rights and sponsorship deals. For instance, a corporate sponsor might request guaranteed mentions of its name in connection with the team across all media, current or future, while the team would want to specify the specific media forms involved to allow room for other potential sponsorship opportunities and prevent conflicting rights with different sponsors due to ambiguous contract language.

510. Early termination clauses should also be carefully drafted. In the context of normal endorsement agreements, the misconduct of high-profile players or even supporters has the potential to prompt the sponsoring company to consider terminating the sponsorship agreement. However, in situations where the naming rights sponsor partner undergoes bankruptcy proceedings, the stadium owner may choose to sever ties with them and disassociate themselves from the sponsorship agreement.

511. In Hong Kong, the majority of sponsorships are determined by the free market and contracts. However, there are also a few legal restrictions in place. For instance, the implementation of the Smoking (Public Health) Ordinance (Cap. 371) in 1982 has led to a gradual prohibition of tobacco advertising, promotion, and sponsorship. This means that tobacco advertisements on TV, radio, printed media, and the internet, as well as display advertisements, have been banned.

§2. Gaming Deals

512. Sports games stand as one of the most highly sought-after genres in the global video gaming landscape. In the Asia-Pacific region alone, sports games amassed around USD 10.59 billion in revenue during 2023.[309] In particular, the online football gaming market has experienced substantial growth with the emergence of highly popular gaming series such as EA Sports FC, formerly recognized as the FIFA series.

513. Barcode Footballer is a mobile football business simulation game[310] that has partnered with the HKFA to include Hong Kong football team members in the game as characters.

§3. Merchandising

514. It is common for fans to exhibit their team loyalty by wearing t-shirts bearing the team logo when attending matches or games. Sport merchandising is the promotion and sale of products aimed at fostering brand recognition and loyalty among fans. As is the case with other sport-related transactions, general civil law applies.

515. Sports merchandising primarily involves licensing and intellectual property. In most instances, licensing serves as the primary method for conducting merchandising. The successful execution of sports merchandising heavily relies on the strategic licensing of trademarks such as names, logos, taglines, and flags associated with teams, events or leagues.

516. In Hong Kong, a trademark can be either registered or unregistered. However, only the owners of a registered trademark, which is registered under the Trade Marks Ordinance (Cap. 559), can enjoy legal protection. One should note that a foreign-registered trademark does not receive protection under the Ordinance in Hong Kong if it is not registered in Hong Kong.

517. In the Hong Kong case *SGG Lisco LLC v. USA Stbading Sports Ltd,*[311] the Defendant is a Hong Kong company, with the name "USA STBADING SPORTS LTD," and the Plaintiff is the owner of the renowned "SPALDING" trademark, which produces numerous sporting equipment worldwide. The history of the "SPALDING" trademark originated in 1876 when Mr. AG Spalding retired from his baseball career and opened a sporting goods store in the U.S. The Defendants have no reasonable explanation nor meaning for the words "STBADING," and the court held that the Defendants could not have come up with this name which resembled "SPALDING" independently, and thus decided that the Defendant is liable for trademark infringement under the Trade Marks Ordinance. This shows that trademarks in sports merchandise are protected by the Trade Marks Ordinance in Hong Kong.

309. https://www.statista.com/statistics/1450979/sports-video-games-revenue-worldwide-region/.
310. Ming Cheung and others, "Analyzing the User Inactiveness in a Mobile Social Game" (HKUST), https://smedia.hkust.edu.hk/ming/papers/2014CPSComGame.pdf.
311. [2020] HKCU 520.

518. With the advancement of technology, sports merchandising has expanded beyond physical stores at sporting venues. E-commerce allows fans and consumers to conveniently purchase sports merchandise online. Under the Electronic Transactions Ordinance (Cap. 553), electronic records and signatures are recognized and treated with equivalent legal status and enforceability as their paper counterparts.

§4. Ownership of Clubs

I. Sports Franchises

519. Sports franchises are the key to a thriving sports industry, serving as the foundation for professional competition in various sports. These organizations hold ownership rights and operate within leagues, driving the commercial and entertainment aspects of sports. Among others, Hong Kong Sevens operated under Hong Kong China Rugby and Hong Kong Premier League operated under the HKFA are notable examples of Hong Kong-based sports franchises that provide opportunities and competitions for both international and local athletes to showcase their skills at a professional level.

520. In Hong Kong, there are no special rules regarding the acquisition and disposal of sports franchises. Apart from general contract law and intellectual property-related law, potential purchasers may undergo a meticulous evaluation process regarding the financial health and value of the franchise, the market potential, brand recognition, fan base, stadium or arena arrangements and any existing contractual obligations. It should be noted that the liability, including debt, will follow the sports franchises to the new owner.

521. However, the disposal of sports franchises or the dissolution of a sports team can give rise to a range of legal considerations. Existing agreements with professional teams and clubs, broadcasters, sponsors and other stakeholders may need to be terminated or modified, leading to a potential breach of contract. Compliance issues including employment law and consumer protection may also come into play. Since most of the sports franchises are limited liability companies, the Companies (Winding Up and Miscellaneous Provisions) Ordinance (Cap. 32) (WUMPO) will apply.

II. Professional Clubs and Teams

522. In the realm of sports, professional clubs and teams are valuable assets.

523. Much like the acquisition of sports franchises, the acquisition of professional clubs and teams also requires a comprehensive commercial evaluation and due diligence process. In particular, the potential purchaser will have to pay attention to the contractual obligations and terms of the athletes' existing agreements and any potential termination clauses that may affect the feasibility of retaining the athletes. It is imperative to ensure that star athletes, who not only contribute to the team's on-field success but also hold significant commercial and marketing value, remain part of the team following the acquisition.

524. However, it is important to exercise caution when acquiring professional clubs and teams, as the purchase could involve either buying the clubs and teams as a business or purchasing shares of the club and team. This means that the sale could be conducted either by the company that owns the club/team or by the shareholders.

525. Where the acquisition takes place through a share transfer, all aspects of the business associated with the professional clubs and teams, including athlete contracts and liabilities, remain unchanged. When professional clubs and teams operate solely as a business under a company, the process can become complicated. Each asset associated with the clubs and teams must be individually transferred. Existing contracts, particularly those with athletes, may need to be renewed, necessitating new consent from the athletes involved. The new owner will also be subjected to section 3 of the Transfer of Business (Protection of Creditors) Ordinance (Cap. 49), and become liable for all the relevant debts and obligations.

526. If professional clubs and teams are established as limited companies within the scope defined by section 2 of the WUMPO, they may wind up in accordance with the WUMPO. However, if they are not structured as such, the owner(s) may bear personal liability for all obligations and liability.

§5. COPYRIGHT ISSUES RELATED TO SPORTS

I. Copyright of Sports Games

527. Copyright is an automatic right guaranteed under Hong Kong law.[312] Pursuant to section 2(1) of the Copyright Ordinance (Cap. 528), an item capable of being protected by copyright can include: (a) original literary, dramatic, musical or artistic works; (b) sound recordings, films, broadcasts or cable programs; and (c) the typographical arrangement of published editions.

528. Movements are generally not protected by copyright. Therefore, the mere act of playing a sport will not usually be afforded protection under the Copyright Ordinance. However, a work of dance or mime can be protected.

312. There have been discussions to create a register for copyrighted works, but changes to the current law remain to be seen.

II. Broadcasting of Sports Events

529. Broadcasts are protected by the Copyright Ordinance. Broadcasts are defined in section 8(1) of the Copyright Ordinance to mean a transmission by wireless telegraphy of sounds or of visual images and sounds or of representations thereof which: (a) is capable of being lawfully received by members of the public in Hong Kong or elsewhere; or (b) is transmitted for presentation to members of the public in Hong Kong or elsewhere, otherwise than through a service for making works or fixations of performances available to the public.

530. Meanwhile, the organizers of major sports competitions tend to assert their copyright and other rights over footage of the sports events they organize through media guidelines and other means.

531. In the case of *Federation Internationale de Football Association & Anor v. The Eatery Ltd,*[313] the Plaintiffs, FIFA and its exclusive licensee in Hong Kong, filed a case against The Eatery Ltd. The Plaintiffs held the exclusive broadcasting rights in Hong Kong and claimed The Eatery Ltd of broadcasting the 2006 FIFA World Cup without a proper license. The lower court ruled in favor of the Plaintiffs and found that the Defendant infringed the Plaintiffs' broadcast rights and copyrights. The court in this case dismissed the Defendant's appeal.

III. Copyright Infringement of Sports Broadcasts

532. In the case of *TBV v. HK Cable,*[314] Television Broadcasts Ltd (TVB) sued HK Cable for copyright infringement. HK Cable retransmitted TVB's broadcasts to its subscribers between July and September 2004. TVB sought summary judgment, arguing there was no valid defense. HK Cable claimed defenses based on the Copyright Ordinance and public interest but failed to convince the court. The court ruled that HK Cable altered the original broadcast by stripping stereo sound, which did not qualify for exemption under the Copyright Ordinance. As a result, TVB's copyright was deemed infringed, and the court ruled in favor of TVB.

533. With the emergence of new media platforms, there is a high chance of violating broadcasting rights or copyright. For instance, individuals may relay the live broadcast through online live-streaming video.

IV. The Trademarks Disputes, Unfair Competition Disputes Issue

534. According to section 3(1) of the Trade Marks Ordinance (Cap. 559), trademark means any sign which is capable of distinguishing the goods or services of

313. [2007] HKCU 1372.
314. [2005] HKCU 15.

one undertaking from those of other undertakings and which is capable of being represented graphically.[315] According to section 3(2) of the Trade Marks Ordinance, trademarks can consist of words, indications, designs, letters, characters, numerals, figurative elements, colors, sounds, smells, the shape of goods or their packaging and any combination of such signs.

535. Even using certain trademarks as keywords for Internet search engines can violate the Trade Marks Ordinance.

536. National emblems and emblems of certain international organizations are the absolute grounds for refusal of registration of trademarks.[316]

537. According to the Olympic Charter, the Olympic symbol, flag, motto, anthem, and other Olympic identifications, designations, Olympic flame and torch are all "Olympic Properties," and all rights belong to the IOC exclusively for all profit-making purposes.[317] The IOC proactively files trademarks, etc., strictly manages its intellectual property rights, ensuring that only official sponsors are permitted to use the Olympic symbols and logos, etc.

538. When companies that are not official licensees or sponsors of major sports events such as the Olympics and the FIFA World Cup create the impression that they are official licensees or sponsors, in order to maximize their marketing and promotional effects, this marketing technique can be related to trademark infringement, which is called "Ambush Marketing."

539. The abovementioned kind of marketing may violate the Trade Marks Ordinance. For example, in the case *ABG Juicy Couture, LLC* (Substituted by the Order of the Honorable Mr. Justice L Chan dated November 19, 2013) *v. Bella International Ltd T/A Juicy Girl & Ors*, the court found that Bella International had infringed upon ABG Juicy Couture's trademarks, violating the Trade Marks Ordinance by using the "Juicy Girl" mark, which closely resembled "Juicy Couture," leading to consumer confusion and violation of the Trade Marks Ordinance.[318]

V. eSports Issues

540. Sound recordings are protected by the Copyright Ordinance,[319] and sound recordings are defined as: (a) a recording of sounds, from which the sounds may be reproduced; or (b) a recording of the whole or any part of a literary, dramatic or musical work, from which sounds reproducing the work or part may be produced, regardless of the medium on which the recording is made or the method by which

315. Section 3(1) Trade Marks Ordinance (Cap. 559).
316. Sections 11, 64–65 Trade Marks Ordinance (Cap. 559).
317. "Protecting the Olympic Properties." August 2016, WIPO Magazine, World Intellectual Property Organization (A United Nations Agency).
318. [2014] HKCU 2094.
319. Section 2(1)(b) Copyright Ordinance (Cap. 528).

the sounds are reproduced or produced.[320] The copyright for audiovisual works of the game can be included within the definition in section 2(1)(b) of the Copyright Ordinance. Alternatively, audiovisual works can be interpreted as a type of film, which is regulated by section 7(1) of the Copyright Ordinance, so the audiovisual works of the game may be protected by copyright laws in Hong Kong.

541. In *Atari Incorporated and Others v. Video Technology Ltd and Others,*[321] copyrights for video games are recognized. Atari was a leading company in the video game industry during the 1970s and 1980s, and Video Technology Ltd is a company that manufactures and sells video games and related technology. Atari claimed that Video Technology was unlawfully copying Atari's copyrighted material and selling it as their own. The court partially upheld Atari's claims, ruling that Video Technology did infringe on Atari's copyright. This case provided a framework for addressing copyright infringement in the video game industry and other fields involving complex digital and creative content. The importance of protecting original works, ensuring fair competition, and preventing consumer deception was emphasized in this case.

eSports related cases

542. Esports involves broadcasting famous players playing games, which is protected by copyright. Before esports became popular, there was a case where the question of whether broadcasting games violated the game developer's copyright was first discussed.

543. The Hong Kong case of *Emagist Entertainment Ltd v. Nether Games (Hong Kong) Ltd and Others*[322] was a copyright infringement case concerning source code by the creators of the game which started another company after creating the game for the Plaintiff. In the end, the court held that the video game source codes belonged to the Plaintiff, and awarded USD 456,000 to the plaintiff as damages from the defendants, who had created the game in the first place. A key issue in the dispute was the legal relationship between the parties involved. If the court had determined that the parties were in a partnership, it would likely have concluded that there was shared ownership of the copyright, as well as shared profits and losses from the game. However, if the defendants were classified as employees of Emagist, it was probable that the copyright would have been attributed to Emagist as the employer. Ultimately, the court ruled that no partnership existed, noting that the defendants had not inquired about their share in the partnership or joint venture, nor had they requested a distribution of profits when the game achieved success.

320. Section 6 Copyright Ordinance (Cap. 528).
321. [1982] HKC 504.
322. [2022] HKCU 1402.

VI. Patents

544. According to the Patents Ordinance (Cap. 514), there are four requirements for grant of a patent: (1) Patentable inventions, (2) Novelty, (3) Inventive step, (4) Industrial application.[323] If the four requirements are all met, the right to patent belongs to the inventor.

VII. Royalty

545. Intellectual property can be licensed to other parties for their authorized use. Generally, there are two types of licenses: exclusive license and non-exclusive license. In conjunction with a licensing fee, royalties may be charged as well, and are usually determined by a formulaic calculation, all of which should be clearly set out in the terms and conditions of the agreement.

546. It is important to ensure that the agreements clearly set out the items that are to be licensed and the related charges.

§6. Anti-competition

I. Broadcasting Rights

547. In Hong Kong, broadcasting rights of major international sports events (including the World Cup finals and NBA Games) in Hong Kong have all along been awarded through competitive bidding among local television broadcasters, taking into account market forces and commercial considerations.[324]

548. Due to its long-standing commitment to free market principles, low tax rates and minimal government intervention in business affairs, Hong Kong has been consistently ranked as one of the world's freest economies in the Heritage Foundation's Index of Economic Freedom for over twenty-five years.[325] Hong Kong's open trade policies with few barriers to international trade and investment have facilitated the free flow of goods and capital, and its legal system based on the English common law has historically provided strong protection for property rights, further contributing to its high rankings.[326] These all support competitive bidding among local broadcasters with regard to the broadcasting rights of sports events.

---

323. SS.9A-9D Patents Ordinance (Cap. 514).

324. *Broadcasting major sports events*, LCQ19, The Government of the HKSAR Press Releases, https://www.info.gov.hk/gia/general/202404/10/P2024041000210.htm?fontSize=1.

325. *Hong Kong axed from economic freedom index after years at top spot, now ranked 107th as part of China,* Hong Kong Free Press, https://hongkongfp.com/2021/03/04/hong-kong-axed-from-economic-freedom-index-after-years-at-top-spot-now-ranked-107th-as-part-of-china/#:~:text=Hong%20Kong%20has%20been%20ranked,2019%20anti%2Dextradition%20bill%20protests.

326. *Hong Kong once again ranked as the world's freest economy,* The Government of the HKSAR Press Releases, https://www.info.gov.hk/gia/general/202209/08/P2022090800841.htm.

549. Under exceptional circumstances, however, the government would have special arrangements with regard to the procurement of broadcasting rights for the Olympic Games, the highest-level major international sports events in the world.

550. In 2021, in view of the unprecedented impact of the COVID-19 pandemic in Hong Kong, the government took exception to secure the broadcasting rights of the Tokyo Olympic Games after it had become clear that all of the broadcasters had ended their discussion for purchasing the rights with a view to "ensuring that the public would have wide access to the coverage of the Tokyo Olympic Games on television free of charge, especially for all events competed by Hong Kong athletes, and that the public can support and cheer for them."[327]

551. In 2024, considering the unfavorable market environment for commercial broadcasters to invest substantially in the broadcasting rights for the Paris Olympic Games, and the social value brought by the prior broadcasting of the Tokyo Olympic Games, the government also decided to cover the full cost of the broadcasting rights for the Paris Olympic Games and Paralympic Games, while the participating broadcasters are to bear the full production costs and bear responsibility for certain obligations, including the production of publicity/promotional programs for the games as well as for promoting sports development in Hong Kong.[328]

552. In the ever-evolving landscape of sports broadcasting, the competition among local broadcasters for exclusive rights to sports events may lead to practices that can undermine the very essence of fair competition. To protect the interests of viewers and ensure diverse and equitable access to sporting events, it is imperative to establish clear and unequivocal rules governing anti-competitive behavior among broadcasters. Without such regulations, we risk creating an environment where monopolistic practices prevail, limiting viewers' choices and inflating costs to advertisers and, ultimately, consumers.

553. The Competition Commission is the key regulator of competition law in Hong Kong, and the main law is the Competition Ordinance (Cap. 619) which came into full effect in December 2015.

554. With regard to the broadcasting market, the legislative framework set out in the Broadcasting Ordinance (the "**BO**") contains express provisions to ensure fair and effective competition in the television program service market.[329] The BO empowers the Communications Authority to enforce the provisions prohibiting the abuse of a dominant position and the use of anti-competitive conduct.

---

327. *Promoting sports development*, The Government of the HKSAR Press Releases, Jul. 21, 2021, https://www.info.gov.hk/gia/general/202107/21/P2021072100392.htm?fontSize=1.

328. *Broadcasting major sports events*, LCQ19, The Government of the HKSAR Press Releases, https://www.info.gov.hk/gia/general/202404/10/P2024041000210.htm?fontSize=1.

329. Guidelines to the Application of the Competition Provisions of the Broadcasting Ordinance, Communications Authority, https://www.coms-auth.hk/filemanager/common/policies_regulations/cop/guideline_competition_e.pdf.

555. Sections 13 and 14 of the BO contains two main anti-competition prohibitions:

a. a prohibition of anti-competitive conduct which has the purpose or effect of preventing, distorting or substantially restricting competition in a television program service market; and
b. a prohibition on the abuse of a dominant position which has the purpose or effect of preventing, distorting or substantially restricting competition in a television program service market.

556. Regarding both prohibitions, the Communications Authority is required to apply a test when assessing potential liability in the Ordinance to see whether the licensee's conduct has the purpose or effect of preventing, distorting or substantially restricting competition in a television program service market.

II. Competition Issues in Membership Admission of Associations

557. The Competition Concerns Regarding Certain Admission Criteria and Procedures of Trade, Sporting, Professional and Industry Associations/Bodies issued by the Bulletin on July 29, 2021,[330] highlighted that although trade associations can positively impact Hong Kong's economy, their decisions regarding membership admission could raise competition issues. The Bulletin emphasized that overly restrictive or discriminatory admission rules may limit market access, reduce competition and potentially violate the Competition Ordinance. Some of the key concerns of the Bulletin included the lack of transparency in decision-making processes, subjective or unclear criteria and rules that disproportionately favor existing members over new entrants, therefore advising associations to ensure fair, objective and transparent admission procedures with clear communications of reasons for rejecting applications, also encouraging associations to review and adjust their practices in order to comply with the Competition Ordinance. In addition, the Bulletin warned that anti-competitive admission practices could lead to investigation and enforcement.

§7. Gambling

558. Sports gambling is a substantial market within the sports landscape. In Hong Kong, the Home and Youth Affairs Bureau holds the responsibility of developing gambling policies and overseeing their execution.

---

330. Competition concerns regarding certain admission criteria and procedures of trade, sporting, professional and industry associations/bodies, Competition Commission, https://www.compcomm.hk/en/media/reports_publications/files/Advisory_Bulletin_on_Trade_Association_Membership_Eng.pdf.

559. Owing to the restrictive approach adopted by the Home and Youth Affairs Bureau toward formulating gambling policy, such policies in Hong Kong are stringent as they confine gambling opportunities to a narrow selection of authorized and regulated establishments. Pursuant to the Gambling Ordinance (Cap. 148), all forms of gambling are illegal unless explicitly authorized by the government under the Betting Duty Ordinance (Cap. 108), licensed by designated public officers appointed by the Secretary for Home and Youth Affairs, or exempted under section 3 of the Gambling Ordinance.

560. In general, the only authorized forms of sports gambling in Hong Kong are horse racing and football betting that are exclusively operated by the HKJC under the Gambling Ordinance. It may also take place on social occasions at licensed restaurants under the Public Health and Municipal Services Ordinance (Cap. 132), premises with authorized liquor sales, or clubhouses that meet the conditions outlined in section 4(2) of the Clubs (Safety of Premises) Ordinance (Cap. 376). Alternatively, placing bets on sporting activities with a bookmaker, websites registered overseas but not in Hong Kong, or in a place other than an authorized gambling establishment would be considered illegal. Horse racing is the most popular sports betting activity in Hong Kong. Horse racing attracts a large number of local and international gamblers. HKJC provides both online and offline betting services. HKJC offers football betting on the Hong Kong Premier League, England Premier League, UEFA Champions League and the World Cup. These events attract a significant number of local and international gamblers. The betting options provided by the Jockey Club include outcome predictions (e.g., win, lose, draw), score predictions, corner counts, and total goals. Illegal betting exists and usually occurs through online platforms or underground gambling networks. The Hong Kong police and the ICAC have been fighting against illegal gambling activities through anti-gambling operations. Recent cases include:

Hong Kong Premier League Match-Fixing Case (May 2023)
ICAC "Green Grass" Operation (February 2024)
ICAC "Tenacity" Operation (May 2024)
Police Anti-Illegal Gambling Operation (July 2024)

Part VI. Recovery of Sports Post-COVID-19

Introduction

561. In Hong Kong, sports had been significantly impacted during the COVID-19 pandemic. The government has implemented various measures and restrictions to curb the spread of the virus, which have had implications for sports events, competitions, and training activities. Many sporting events have been either cancelled or postponed minimizing the risk of transmission. Additionally, sports facilities, gyms, and training centers have had to adhere to strict health and safety protocols, such as temperature checks, social distancing measures, and enhanced cleaning procedures. Athletes and sports organizations have had to adapt to these new norms and challenges, finding innovative ways to continue training and competing while prioritizing the health and well-being of participants.

562. Due to the COVID-19 pandemic, the government had implemented various epidemic prevention measures to contain the spread of the virus, which had a substantial impact on local sports. Numerous sporting competitions and events have been canceled or postponed indefinitely. Despite the above, the government commissioned advertisements to encourage the public to do more exercise. Although the pandemic brought about the closure of a lot of public sports facilities across Hong Kong, the government encouraged the public to engage in sports activities with proper social distancing measures, such as the use of the "LeaveHomeSafe" application before entering sports venues.[331]

563. A general approach of full-scale closure of sporting facilities was adopted to reduce social contact and contain the spread of the virus, with the main exception of amenity areas which remained open to the public. Large-scale events involving the general public such as the Jockey Club Vitality Run and the Hong Kong Games were also subject to cancellation.

564. For instance, under the Compulsory Quarantine of Certain Persons Arriving at Hong Kong from Foreign Places Regulation (Cap. 599E), the Hong Kong Government closed the border and barred all incoming travelers from entering the

331. LCSD (Oct. 29, 2021), https://www.lcsd.gov.hk/clpss/en/webApp/NewsDetails.do?id=16036 , accessed Apr. 12, 2024.

city. This limited Hong Kong's ability to host international sporting events and limited foreign athletes' ability to visit. Moreover, the inclusion of mandatory testing and mask-wearing regulations. These regulations were previously in force during 2020-2022, but as of early 2023, these restrictions were relaxed or lifted.

565. As the health and safety of the public is paramount, COVID-19 and the measures taken during this period limited Hong Kong's citizens from fully participating in sports during the height of the pandemic. Having said that, the government and sports organizations have adopted all possible measures to maximize the possibility for citizens to enjoy sports during the pandemic.

§1. Governmental Measures During COVID-19

566. The Hong Kong government is primarily responsible for Hong Kong's anti-epidemic regulations, as seen by the Amendment regulations made under section 8 of the Prevention and Control of Disease Ordinance (Cap. 599).

567. The LCSD announced in December 2020 that, in view of the situation of COVID-19, the following measures had to be adopted to achieve social distancing:

a. Some leisure and cultural venues/facilities including all public swimming pools and water sports centers managed by the LCSD were temporarily closed. Lifeguard services at those gazetted beaches which were originally open during the winter period, including Deep Water Bay Beach, Clear Water Bay Second Beach, Silverstrand Beach and Golden Beach, were suspended as well. Showering facilities and changing rooms at all gazetted beaches were also closed to reduce the chances of spreading the virus.
b. Non-fee-charging and fee-charging venues for team games including hard-surface soccer pitches, grass pitches, baseball courts, rugby pitches, cricket grounds, basketball courts, volleyball courts, netball courts, handball courts, hockey grounds and a roller hockey court were temporarily closed to avoid crowd gathering. These facilities were cordoned off gradually. In addition, the LCSD also temporarily closed some leisure facilities such as spectator stands, and billiard facilities and stepped up cleaning measures. At the same time, dancing activities were temporarily prohibited in indoor facilities and some leisure facilities such as barbecue sites, indoor children's playrooms and Pui O Campsite were closed as well.
c. Some indoor and outdoor sports premises under the LCSD continued to be open for sub-group training/classes with not more than two persons in each sub-group. For sub-group training/classes in activity rooms, multi-purpose rooms, and dance rooms, no more than two persons were allowed in each sub-group including the coach (only one-on-one classes are allowed). Each sub-group must be at least 1.5 meters apart or with effective partitions in between. Members of the public were required to wear a mask before and after exercise at outdoor leisure venues and wear a mask at all times at indoor leisure venues.

d. Further, processing and acceptance of booking applications for dancing activities in indoor facilities, public swimming pools and water sports centers, as well as the use of amphitheaters and leisure venues for non-designated use, sales activities at non-fee-charging leisure venues, and school/group booking applications for road safety towns were also suspended.[332]

568. LCSD staff, together with law enforcement teams of relevant departments, stepped up patrols during the Christmas holiday of 2020. Nearly 6,000 times verbal advice and ten fixed penalty notices were given out between December 24 and 26 of 2020.[333]

569. The LCSD announced in October 2021 the arrangement of using the "LeaveHomeSafe" mobile application before entering LCSD offices and venues starting from November 1, 2021. Except for exempted persons, all persons would be required to use the app to scan the venue QR code before they were allowed to enter LCSD offices and venues.[334]

570. In view of the COVID-19 pandemic, the LCSD had canceled different sports-related events such as the Jockey Club Vitality Run of the 8th Hong Kong Games scheduled to be held in March 2022,[335] and the 8th Hong Kong Games to avoid people gathering and to reduce social contact, thus decreasing the risk of spreading COVID-19 in the community and safeguarding public health.[336]

571. The Education Bureau published the COVID-19 Health Protection Measures for Schools which include the following measures:

a. Students having received two doses of COVID-19 vaccines for more than fourteen days may participate in extra-curricular sports activities.
b. All participants, except students, who hold a "COVID-19 Medical Exemption Certificate" must present a negative COVID-19 test result proof conducted within seven days.
c. All participants are required to complete Rapid Antigen Test (RAT) on the same day and before attending the event.

---

332. LCSD, "Latest arrangements for LCSD public services," Press Release, Dec. 1, 2020, accessed Mar. 1, 2024, available at https://www.lcsd.gov.hk/clpss/en/webApp/NewsDetails.do?id=15188.
333. LCSD, "LCSD appeals to public not to gather during holidays," Press Release, Dec. 26, 2020, accessed Mar. 1, 2024, available at https://www.lcsd.gov.hk/clpss/en/webApp/NewsDetails.do?id=15218.
334. LCSD, "Use of 'LeaveHomeSafe' mobile app required on entering LCSD offices and venues starting Nov. 1," Press Release, Oct. 29, 2021, accessed Mar. 3, 2024, available at https://www.lcsd.gov.hk/clpss/en/webApp/NewsDetails.do?id=16036.
335. LCSD, "Jockey Club Vitality Run of 8th Hong Kong Games cancelled," Press Release, Feb. 11, 2022, accessed Mar. 3, 2024, available at https://www.lcsd.gov.hk/clpss/en/webApp/NewsDetails.do?id=16307.
336. LCSD. "8th Hong Kong Games cancelled." Press Release, Apr. 1, 2022, accessed Mar. 1, 2024, available at: https://www.lcsd.gov.hk/clpss/en/webApp/NewsDetails.do?id=16359.

d. All participants are required to submit the "Health Declaration Form" on each event day and to observe the anti-epidemic measures/special arrangements of respective events.

572. The Hong Kong Sports Alliance's survey in 2020 found that 67% of the coaches lost 100% of their income due to the pandemic, while 60% had to work part-time jobs to make ends meet. Former Chief Executive Carrie Lam Cheng Yuet-ngor revealed a relief package in 2020 to help sports coaches affected by the coronavirus outbreak. They would receive a one-off grant of HKD 7,500. The scheme was implemented via NSAs and Sports Organizations. Community sports schools as well as other sports clubs could also apply for financial assistance as individual businesses if their operation has been affected by the pandemic with a maximum of HKD 100,000 subsidy per unit.[337]

573. Hong Kong's top athletes were assured financial support despite the lack of competitions for evaluation because of the COVID-19 pandemic. Medal winners at the Tokyo Olympics received improved support to Elite A level, who could receive a maximum of HKD 48,000 per month. Moreover, those who registered strong performances at the Tokyo Olympic Games would attain a higher status under the elite training grant scheme in accordance with their results.[338]

574. The LCSD has also introduced the Pilot Scheme on Subvention for New Sports in mid-2021[339] to support the development of new sports in Hong Kong and aims to provide more opportunities and choices for the public to do more physical exercise.

§2. Measures Undertaken by Sports Associations (Federations, Leagues, Clubs)

575. The measures taken by Sports Associations are consistent with the government's regulations. Hong Kong's sport organizations have attempted to provide support for those affected by the COVID-19 pandemic.

576. Besides the government's measures, Hong Kong's sports associations have also implemented similar measures to prevent the spread of the virus. For example,

337. Chan Kin-wa, Sports coaches to receive one-off subsidy of HKD 7,500 from the government's latest Anti-epidemic Fund, South China Morning Post (Apr. 8, 2020 8:58 pm), https://www.scmp.com/sport/hong-kong/article/3079052/sports-coaches-receive-one-subsidy-hk7500-under-governments-latest.
338. Chan Kin-wa, Hong Kong elite athletes' financial support to remain for next year despite lack of competition for evaluation due to COVID-19 pandemic, South China Morning Post (Oct. 5, 2021 5:56 pm).
339. LCSD (May 31, 2021), *Pilot Scheme on Subvention for New Sports opens for application*, https://www.lcsd.gov.hk/clpss/en/webApp/NewsDetails.do?id=15493, accessed Apr. 11, 2024.

the Hong Kong Schools Sports Federation suspended all sporting events during 2020,[340] while additional anti-epidemic measures for inter-school sporting events were implemented during 2021-2022.

577. Despite this, the HKJC had attempted to provide support for those affected by the COVID-19 pandemic. This is notable with the organization's introduction of the "Jockey Club Long COVID Rehabilitation Programme," which provides support to people recovering from COVID-19, particularly vulnerable groups in the community.

578. Similarly, the Hong Kong Premier League canceled their 2021-2022 season to reduce the spread of the virus. The League further adopted anti-epidemic measures in accordance with the relevant epidemic prevention regulations, including regular rapid antigen testing, mask-wearing except when exercising outdoors and arranging separate rooms for team meals, etc.

579. Hong Kong Football Club also imposed a list of measures during the pandemic period. They include, without limitation, temperature checking upon entry to club premises; closure of sports and recreational facilities; temporary suspension of reciprocal club members from accessing club premises; temporary closure of the club's food and beverage outlets; and imposing a maximum gathering limit of two people.

580. The first wave of the COVID-19 outbreak oversaw a complete suspension of the HKFA fixtures and training sessions alike before preventive measures were loosened in 2021, and matches were allowed to be played behind closed doors in designated LCSD venues. During this challenging time of the COVID-19 pandemic, the HKFA worked with the Hong Kong government regarding relief measures, in order to reduce the impact for Hong Kong Premier League clubs. The HKFA notified the clubs about the successful application in getting funding support from the Home Affairs Bureau, which would be provided to the HKFA in order to enable the HKFA to waive the competition fees for the closed-door matches and pitch rental charges for training sessions by Hong Kong Premier League clubs in February and March 2020.[341]

581. Since the 2020-21 BOC Life Hong Kong Premier League had been postponed for more than two months since December 2020 due to the pandemic situation, there was not sufficient time for the rest of matches for the 2020-21 season.

340. Joanne Ma, Coronavirus Outbreak: All HKSSF Sports Events Suspended, South China Morning Post (Feb. 3, 2020 12:19 pm).

341. HKFA, "HKFA Relief Measures and Applied Funding Support from HAB to Support Clubs," Press Release, May 5, 2020, accessed Mar. 3, 2024, available at https://www.hkfa.com/en/news/latest-news/17870/detail.

In view of this, the HKFA had reached an agreement with clubs and relevant parties and announced that the 2020-21 HKFA Senior Shield, FA Cup and Reserve Division league would be canceled.[342]

582. The government announced on January 4, 2022, that, with effect on February 24, 2022, users of scheduled premises regulated under the Prevention and Control of Disease (Requirements and Directions) (Business and Premises) Regulation (Cap. 599F) and cultural and leisure facilities under the LCSD were required to have received at least one dose of COVID-19 vaccine for entry. The government further elaborated that the relevant requirement would be implemented through a vaccine pass. In this regard, the "LeaveHomeSafe" mobile app was enhanced to facilitate venue operators in checking whether users have complied with relevant vaccination requirements.[343]

583. The Hong Kong Cricket Club had, during COVID-19, imposed mandatory mask-wearing within club facilities when not at the dining table. There was also a maximum group size limit for guests at twelve people.

584. In light of the ongoing COVID-19 pandemic and to ensure the health and safety of swimmers and staff, the Hong Kong Amateur Swimming Association announced its decision to cancel the New World Harbour Race 2020. Where the government suspended swimming facilities such as public pools and water sports centers, large-scale public swimming events and other association-held swimming competitions of various categories were also canceled by the Hong Kong Amateur Swimming Association.[344]

585. In view of the novel coronavirus pandemic, the Hong Kong Basketball Association decided to postpone the 2020 Hong Kong Basketball Silver Medal Game and the Hong Kong Basketball League, which were originally scheduled to start in early April 2020.[345]

§3. Post-pandemic Outlook

586. To conclude, the impact of the pandemic has led to numerous measures being taken in Hong Kong to combat the virus, with local sport organizations also

342. HKFA, "Arrangement of 2020-21 BOC Life Hong Kong Premier League and Sapling Cup Match Resumption," Press Release, Feb. 12, 2021, accessed Mar. 3, 2024, available at https://www.hkfa.com/en/news/latest-news/18137/detail.
343. HKFA, "Introduction of 'Vaccine Pass' by the government," Press Release, Jan. 31, 2022, accessed Mar. 3, 2024, available at https://www.hkfa.com/en/news/latest-news/18984/detail.
344. Hong Kong Amateur Swimming Association, "New World Harbour Race 2020 Cancelled due to COVID-19 Pandemic," Press Release, Jul. 17, 2020, accessed Mar. 3, 2024, available at https://hkgswimming.org.hk/en/viewfile/?file=dXBsb2FkL3RlbXBsYXRlLzI5MTYvcGRmX2ZpbGVzXzEvNWYxMTU0ZDBhODZmOC5wZGY=.
345. Basketball Association of Hong Kong, China, "香港籃球銀牌賽及香港籃球聯賽延期通知" Announcement, Oct. 3, 2020, accessed Mar. 3, 2024, available at http://basketball.org.hk/index.php/latestnews/806-2020-03-03-02-21-54.

joining in to support these efforts. Although the anti-epidemic measures have temporarily impacted the local sports scene, it is certain that after the pandemic, Hong Kong's sports culture will continue to thrive once more.

587. The COVID-19 pandemic has significantly impacted the sports industry in Hong Kong. From the suspension of events and competitions to the implementation of strict health and safety protocols, athletes, coaches, and sports organizations have faced unprecedented challenges. Despite these obstacles, the resilience and adaptability of the sports community have been evident. After the pandemic, the government immediately introduced measures to support the resumption of different sports events and also provided government subsidies and financial support schemes to the sports industry in Hong Kong. The government made it clear in a statement in 2021 that it fully supports the development of sports in Hong Kong.[346]

588. As we look toward the future, it is clear that the pandemic has reshaped the landscape of sports in Hong Kong, emphasizing the importance of flexibility, technology integration, and community support in ensuring the continued growth and development of the industry. By learning from the lessons of this challenging period, the sports sector in Hong Kong can emerge stronger, more connected, and better equipped to thrive in a post-pandemic world.

346. HK Government (Sep. 15, 2021), https://www.info.gov.hk/gia/general/202109/15/P2021091500396.htm, accessed on Apr. 12, 2024.

Part VII. The Future of Sports

589. The Hong Kong Law Society has formed a specialized Sports Law Committee to advance legal practice in the sports sector. During the Council's visit to Beijing in April 2024, they met with the General Administration of Sport of China, discussing how the expertise of Hong Kong's legal profession can be leveraged for the National Games 2025.

590. Furthermore, the Hong Kong Law Society recognized that law and sports intersect in a number of ways. Apart from sports dispute resolution, the Law Society pointed out that lawyers can cover a much wider range of legal issues in the sports industry. The increase in private equity financing models for sports clubs and federations has led to an increase in demand for legal advice in the sector.[347]

591. Aiming to increase awareness of the various legal issues that can emerge in sports, and how Hong Kong's legal services are prepared to support the city's role as Asia's sports hub, the Hong Kong Law Society will be holding a Sports Law Conference in early 2025.[348]

592. Cross-border investments have played a pivotal role in the remarkable expansion of the sports industry, as foreign capital continues to pour into various segments of the sector. This includes investments in overseas ownership of premier leagues, professional teams, and sponsorship of clubs or competitions. Notably, the global sports market has already reached a sizeable value of USD 512.14 billion in 2023, and it is projected to witness further growth, reaching nearly USD 624 billion by 2027.[349]

593. Similar to many other regions and countries, Hong Kong welcomes cross-border investment in the sports sector. Hong Kong, with its long-standing reputation as an international and cosmopolitan city, has been long recognized for its business-friendly environment, adherence to the rule of law, commitment to free trade, unrestricted flow of information, open and fair competition, and comprehensive financial networks. These factors make Hong Kong an ideal destination for

347. *"Sports and Law,"* July 2024, Hong Kong Lawyer, accessible at https://www.hk-lawyer.org/content/sports-and-law, accessed on Aug. 24, 2024.
348. *Ibid.*
349. "Global Sports Market Analysis: Size, Drivers, Trends, Opportunities And Strategies," Business Research Company (December 2023), https://blog.tbrc.info/2023/12/sports-market-report/ (accessed on Sep. 27, 2024).

investors seeking access to a sophisticated local market. Hong Kong also serves as a vital gateway, enabling investors to expand their reach not only to mainland China but also to global markets.

594. Hong Kong's policy strongly advocates for the principles of free trade and a free market, with limited interference from the government. With the exception of a maximum foreign ownership limit of 49% for businesses applying for specific broadcasting licenses, there are generally no significant restrictions on foreign investment in the region. Under Article 112 of the Basic Law, no foreign exchange control policies shall be applied in Hong Kong. Investors have the freedom to transfer funds to individuals or entities inside or outside Hong Kong through various channels, including dividends, interest, royalties, service fees, and branch profits.

595. The evolving world of sports demands a strategic approach to managing contracts with third parties, especially in light of recent incidents like the Messi incident in Hong Kong. Ensuring clear, fair, and enforceable agreements is crucial for protecting the interests of all parties involved. By establishing robust contract management practices, sports organizations can mitigate risks and prevent miscommunications that lead to public relations crises. As the industry continues to grow, adopting best practices in contract management will not only safeguard reputations but also foster more fruitful partnerships, ultimately enhancing the overall integrity of sports.

596. In conclusion, the landscape of sports today is ripe for transformation, particularly in the realms of funding accountability and monetizing sports. As stakeholders increasingly scrutinize financial practices, it is essential that organizations prioritize transparency and ethical management of funds to foster trust and sustainability.

597. Additionally, the opportunities for monetizing sports—whether through innovative sponsorship models, digital engagement, or enhanced fan experiences—remain vast and underexploited. There is considerable room for improvement in these areas, and by addressing these challenges, the sports industry can unlock its full potential for growth and impact. This is a crucial time for the government to consider putting in place a comprehensive policy for sports and esports development, and the cooperation and contribution of all stakeholders, including various professionals, businesspeople and sporting talent, are of utmost importance in growing this area together.

Selected Bibliography

Print/online Sources

Beale, H.G. and Chitty, J. *Chitty on Contracts: Vol. 1: General Principles* (31st ed. London: Sweet & Maxwell 2012)

Nature and Formation of Agency (Halsbury's Laws of Hong Kong, LexisNexis 2022)

Protecting the Olympic Properties (WIPO Magazine, World Intellectual Property Organization (A United Nations Agency) August 2016)

Zubcic, L., Windholz, E. & Ng, Y-F, *Smashed Vials, Fair Trials? Sun Yang and Procedural Fairness at the CAS* (Int Sports Law J 2023)

Web Sources

Webpages within the following parent websites:

Anti-Doping Organization of Hong Kong, China: https://www.antidoping.hk/

Court of Arbitration for Sports: https://www.tas-cas.org/

Hong Kong Basic Law: https://www.basiclaw.gov.hk/en/basiclaw/index.html

Hong Kong Department of Justice: https://www.doj.gov.hk/en/home/index.html

Hong Kong Immigration Department: https://www.immd.gov.hk/eng/index.html

Hong Kong Independent Commission Against Corruption: https://www.icac.org.hk/en/home/index.html

Hong Kong Inland Revenue Department: https://www.ird.gov.hk/eng/welcome.htm

Hong Kong Jockey Club: https://www.hkjc.com/home/english/index.aspx

Hong Kong Labour Department: https://www.labour.gov.hk/eng/index.htm

Hong Kong Legislative Council: https://www.legco.gov.hk/en/index.html

Hong Kong Leisure and Cultural Services Department: https://www.lcsd.gov.hk/en/index.html

The Football Association of Hong Kong, China Limited: https://www.hkfa.com/en

The Sports Federation & Olympic Committee of Hong Kong, China: https://www.hkolympic.org/

Sports Commission of Hong Kong: https://www.sportscommission.hk/eng/index.htm

World Anti-Doping Agency: https://www.wada-ama.org/en

Index

The numbers here refer to paragraph numbers.

www.ingramcontent.com/pod-product-compliance
Lightning Source LLC
Chambersburg PA
CBHW071345230926
51846CB00002B/453
* 9 7 8 9 4 0 3 5 3 0 8 9 5 *